PATCHWORK QUILTS FOR BEDS

PIPPA ABRAHAMS

Garnet
PUBLISHING

INTRODUCTION

One of the most popular crafts practised today is quiltmaking. The pleasure of working with textiles to create something both decorative and functional creates an absorbing interest that celebrates our existence as individuals. The patterns used in quiltmaking draw on tribal and applied art patterns that are to be found in ancient civilisations throughout the globe. This common inheritance, combined with the enthusiasm and creativity of American quiltmakers, is largely responsible for the popularity of the craft today.

The majority of the designs included in this book are easy enough for a beginner to make. Clear instructions are given in a 'recipe' format with plenty of detailed, step-by-step drawings and full use is made of time-saving cutting and sewing techniques. Part of the pleasure of making a quilt lies in selecting colours and fabrics to create a unique piece of work. Thus the quilt designs are presented in light, medium and dark tones to suggest the placement of colour values. Simple colour schemes are offered to help beginners build their colour confidence. There is also a comprehensive Skill Basics section which offers full details of the construction techniques required to complete the quilts.

QUILTING TERMS

The word **quilt** comes from the French word *cuilte* which is itself derived from the Latin *culcita*, meaning mattress or cushion. So essentially a quilt is a textile sandwich consisting of a top, a filler and a backing. The top layer may consist of patches sewn together in a rhythmic way to create a surface pattern. The three layers of the quilt are then held together with the quilting stitch, which can be sewn either by hand or by machine.

The term **patchwork** traditionally describes either pieced or appliquéd work. Often, and particularly in the quilts in this book, the joined patches create tile patterns which are repeated in a series of blocks to form the quilt top.

Quilt set is the pattern in which the completed blocks are sewn together to form the quilt top. There are countless ways of setting the blocks together and some of the most popular are used in the quilt designs that follow.

The thickness of the **wadding** contributes to the textural pattern created by the quilting stitch when the three layers of the quilt are sewn together. A 2-oz polyester wadding, the most economical choice, is suitable for beginners and is easily laundered. Today, cotton, wool and polyester waddings are available in the following standard sizes for quilt making:

single bed : 60 x 96 inches
double bed: 80 x 96 inches
queen size: 86 x 108 inches
king size: 102 x 108 inches

When purchasing wadding, be sure to order a size which is at least 4 inches larger than your quilt top. For example a 72 x 104-inch top will need a queen size wadding.

The fabric chosen for the **backing** should be of a similar weight to, and in sympathy with the fabrics used to create the top. It often consists of two or three panels of fabric joined together.

For quilting, a wooden quilting hoop will give just as good results as a large traditional quilting frame. Round ones of around 18-inch diameter made especially for quilting are a good choice. They can be supported on the edge of a table or a chair while work is in progress. The hoop should be removed from the quilt overnight to avoid stretching the fabric.

Pippa Abrahams

Important note: a ¼-inch seam allowance is used on all projects in this book, unless otherwise stated.

CONTENTS

LOG CABIN

Brenda Woodward made the richly coloured quilt top from which this design is taken. Log Cabin makes good use of recycled, scrap fabrics. The secret in achieving the strong graphic quality the quilt illustrates is to start by dividing the supply of fabrics into three contrasting piles of light, medium and dark values. The light and dark fabrics are the easiest to identify, and the medium values are more difficult to determine. Stick small swatches of all the chosen fabrics to a sheet of A4 paper and make a photocopy on a black and white copier. The resulting grey scale will quickly identify which medium fabrics will provide sufficient contrast to the light and dark selections.

QUILT SIZE 72 x 96 inches
BLOCK SIZE 12 inches
BLOCKS REQUIRED 24

The Log Cabin blocks are arranged in a straight set to form the centre panel, which is surrounded by three borders. The inner and outer borders are plain strips of fabric. The middle, pieced, border is composed of a series of pieced rectangles. Each rectangle is composed of three pieced triangles that form a pattern unit known as Wild Gees The larger triangle is popularly know as the goose patch, with the tw smaller triangles symbolising the sky.

instructions are given for rotary cutting and speed construction methods using the sewing machine. All seams use a ¼-inch seam allowance. It is important that the ¼-inch seam sewn is precisely the same as the ¼-inch seam cut with your rotary cutter. (See the Skill Basics section, page 68, for an explanation of how to achieve this.) The Log Cabin blocks are speedily completed using a fast strip-piecing sequence and the Wild Geese units of the pieced border are made from a series of rectangles and squares. Read through all the instructions before starting.

Log Cabin

MATERIALS

(based on 42-inch fabric width)
Light fabric: 3 yards
Medium fabric: 3 yards
Dark fabric: 4 yards
Binding fabric: ¾ yard
Backing fabric: 5 ⅓ yards
Vadding: 86 x 108 inches (queen size)

CUTTING

From the dark fabric
Note: be sure to cut the border strips first. Cut them along the straight warp or long grain, parallel to the selvedge, and then put to one side.

1 Inner Border A: cut two strips 3½ x 60½ inches.
2 Inner Border B: cut two strips 3½ x 54½ inches.
3 Outer Border A: cut two strips 3½ x 90½ inches.
4 Outer Border B: cut two strips 3½ x 72½ inches.
   From now on the fabric is cut in strips along the straight weft, or cross grain, at 90° to the selvedge.
5 Log Cabin centres: from 3½-inch strips cut 24 squares 3½ x 3½ inches.
6 Wild Geese units: from 3½-inch strips cut 192 squares 3½ x 3½ inches.

From the medium fabric
1 Log Cabin blocks: cut 34 2-inch strips from selvedge to selvedge.
2 Wild Geese units: from seven 3½-inch strips cut 40 rectangles 3½ x 6½ inches.

From the light fabric:
1 Log Cabin blocks: cut 28 2-inch strips from selvedge to selvedge.
2 Wild Geese units: from 10 3½-inch strips cut 56 rectangles 3½ x 6½ inches.

CONSTRUCTION
Piecing the blocks
The illustrations below show the two types of block required. Block A is a mirror image of Block B. Twelve Block As and twelve Block Bs are required. The blocks are pieced by sewing strips in a regular sequence around the centre square. The first round of strips is the trickiest to sew. To avoid confusion label the sides of each centre square by sticking a piece of masking tape, labelled 1, 2, 3 and 4,

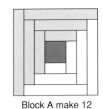

Block A make 12   Block B make 12

onto the back of each one, avoiding the ¼-inch seam allowance.

Unit A   Unit B

To chain piece Block A

1 Label the back of twelve of the centre squares, avoiding the ¼-inch seam allowance, as described above (see illustration above).
2 Place a 2-inch wide strip of light-coloured fabric, right side of the fabric facing upwards, under the foot of the sewing machine. Lower the presser foot and wind the needle down to anchor the fabric.
3 Position the first centre square, right side down, on the strip, so the edge of Side 1 is aligned with the edge of the strip.
4 Set the stitch length to 2.5 and sew the centre square onto the strip. Stop sewing a few stitches beyond the edge of the square and wind the needle in to anchor the fabric. Do not remove the strip from the machine.
5 Place the next centre square, right side down, on the strip, so the edge of Side 1 is aligned with the edge of the strip.
6 Sew the square onto the strip. Stop sewing a few inches beyond the edge of the square and wind the needle down to anchor the fabric. Do not remove the strip from the machine.
7 Repeat the process with two more centre squares. The best results are obtained by sewing no more than four blocks at a time.
8 Remove the fabric from the machine and trim the strip level with each centre square. Press the seams away from the centre square.

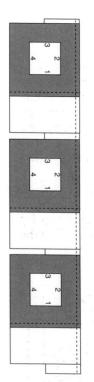

9 Place a 2-inch wide strip of light-coloured fabric, right side of the fabric facing upwards, under the foot of the sewing machine. Lower the presser foot and wind the needle in to anchor the fabric .

10 Position a pressed block, right side down, on the strip, aligning Side 2 to be sewn. Sew the block onto the strip. Stop sewing a few stitches beyond the edge of the block and wind the needle down to anchor the fabric. Do not remove the strip from the machine.

11 Place the next pressed block, right side down, on the strip, aligning Side 2 to be sewn. Sew down and repeat with the next two pressed blocks. Remove from the machine and trim as before. Press the seams away from the centre square.

12 Take a 2-inch strip of medium contrast fabric and anchor it, right side up, under the machine. Position one of the trimmed and pressed blocks with Side 3 aligned at the sewing edge. Sew to the strip and repeat the process with the three other blocks.

13 Remove from the machine and press the seam allowance away from the centre of each block.

14 Using another strip of medium-contrast fabric follow the same steps, sewing Side 4 of the blocks to the strip. Remove from the machine, trim and press each block to complete the first round.

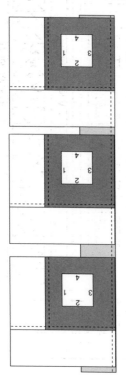

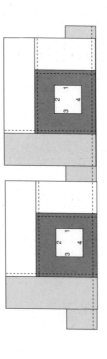

Note: the first round is the trickiest to piece. Notice that two light-coloured strips are always followed by two contrast strips. After the first round is completed the new strip is always sewn onto the side where the two seams meet the edge. Continue adding the strips until the block is complete. Make twelve of Block A.

Two seams meet the edge

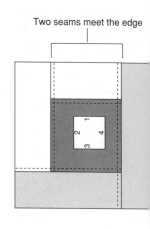

To chain piece Block B

1 Now label the back of twelve of the Block B centi squares (see illustration on page 5), avoiding the ¼-inc seam allowance.

2 Follow the procedure outlined above and chain piece th Block Bs, following the marked piecing sequence.

Piecing the central panel

1 From A and B blocks make twelve of Unit A.

2 From the Unit As make six Unit Bs .

3 Refer to illustration on page 5 and piece together the Unit Bs to complete the centre panel.

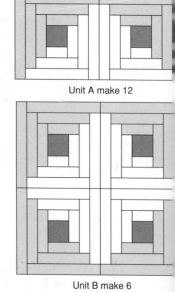

Unit A make 12

Unit B make 6

Piecing the Wild Geese border

The Wild Geese units are made up of three triangles. The large triangle is popularly referred to as the goose triangle with the two smaller triangles beir known as the sky triangles. The simple speed constructic method described uses rectangles cut from strips of fabric ar yields a bonus collection of half-square triangle units th can be saved and used in another project.

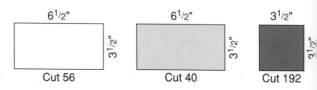

6½" Cut 56   6½" Cut 40   3½" Cut 192

On the wrong side of the dark-coloured 3½ x 3½-inch squares, mark a diagonal line with a fabric marker of your choice. Mark a second line ½ inch to one side of the diagonal.

Place a marked square on a rectangle with right sides together and sew two seams on each marked line, as illustrated.

Cut between the seams. Put the resulting half-square triangle unit to one side. Fold back the remaining sky triangle pressing the seam allowance away from the goose patch.

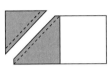

Place a second marked square on the opposite side of the rectangle as illustrated and sew two seams on each of the marked lines.

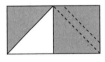

Cut between the two seams. Put the half-square triangle unit to one side. Fold back the remaining sky triangle pressing the seam allowance away from the goose patch, to complete the unit.

Make 56 of Unit C and 40 of Unit D.

Unit C make 56

Unit D make 40

Refer to the quilt top construction diagram (previous page) and make two Pieced Border A strips. For colour value placement of the units refer to page 5.

Note: avoid blunting the point of the goose patches when joining the units together. See below which illustrates how the seam

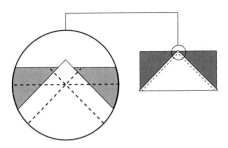

joining the Wild Geese units should track exactly through the X formed by the triangle seams.

8   Refer to the quilt top construction diagram and make two Pieced Border B strips. For colour value placement of the units refer to page 5.

Attaching the borders

Refer to the Skill Basics section, page 70, for help if required.

1   Attach an Inner Border A to either side of the centre panel.

2   Attach an Inner Border B to the top and bottom of the centre panel.

3   Attach a Pieced Border A to each side of the quilt top.

4   Attach a Pieced Border B to the top and bottom.

5   Attach an Outer Border A to either side.

6   Complete the quilt top by attaching an Outer Border B to the top and bottom.

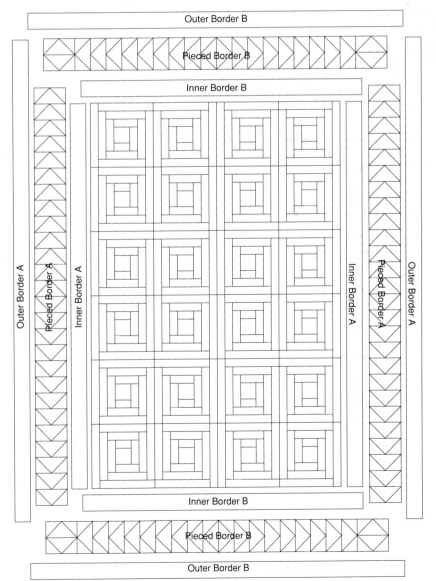

Quilt top construction

Piecing the backing

The following method avoids having a seam running down the centre of the backing:

1. Cut the backing fabric from selvedge to selvedge, into two equal halves.
2. With right sides together join the two halves by sewing ½-inch seams along the selvedges as illustrated, making a large tube.
3. Clip along the seam allowances to release the tension of the selvedges.
4. Place one seam on top of the other, as illustrated, and press along the length of one of the resulting folds.
5. Cut along the pressed crease and open out the backing fabric. A narrow strip of backing fabric now lies on either side of the wide centre panel.

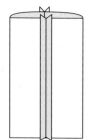
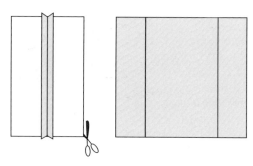

QUILTING AND FINISHING

See the Skill Basics section, page 72, for notes on how to layer and baste the quilt sandwich. Advice is also given on attaching a hanging sleeve and attaching continuous French binding on page 74.

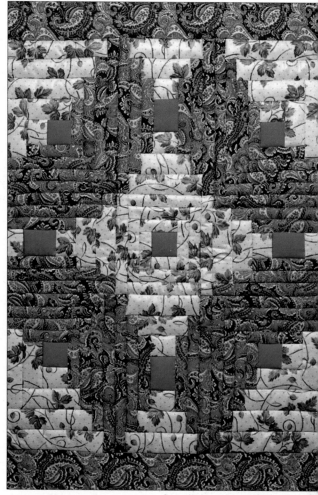

Examples of different Log Cabin colour schemes

DRUNKARD'S PATH

Sophie Popolowska, a gifted needlewoman, made this magnificent quilt. Each block consists of 36 Drunkard's Path pattern units arranged in a mosaic formation. This is just one of the infinite number of arrangements that are possible using the Drunkard's Path pattern unit. The quilt top consists of two sets of block units arranged alternately in a straight set. A row of half blocks is positioned on the top and bottom of the centre panel. The border consists of inner and outer accent strips enclosing a 3-inch middle border section that can be used to show off some quilting. Instead of binding, the edges of the quilt are finished with folded Prairie Points, forming a series of pointed triangles around the perimeter.

QUILT SIZE 85 x 103 inches

BLOCK SIZE 18 inches

BLOCKS REQUIRED 16, plus 8 half sized blocks

Although classified as 'advanced' the curved seams are not so difficult to sew. The secret lies in the accuracy of the templates and the use of balance marks to match the seams. Six fabrics are used in the construction method described. To avoid confusion it helps to stick a small numbered swatch of each fabric onto a piece of A4 paper and to label it. Read through all instructions before starting and refer to the Skill Basics section for detailed instructions on how to sew a perfect curved seam (page 69) and for any other technical help you may require.

Fabric A 5 yards

Fabric B 1 yard

Fabric C 6 yards including 3 yards for Prairie Points

Fabric D 1¾ yards

Fabric E 3 yards

Fabric F ½ yard

CUTTING

Cut the border strips first. Cut along the warp grain, parallel to the selvedge and then put to one side. Caution: the measurements given for the border strips are mathematically correct. It is wise to add 2 inches working allowance to the length given to ensure a good fit when completing the quilt top. See Skill Basics section, page 70, for detailed explanation.

Borders
From Fabric C
1 Inner Border B: cut two strips 1 x 73½ inches
2 Outer Border A: cut two strips 1 x 97½ inches
3 Outer Border B: cut two strips 1 x 80½ inches
From Fabric E
1 Middle Border A: cut two strips 3½ x 91½ inches
2 Middle Border B: cut two strips 3½ x 76½ inches

Make the templates using the three full-size patterns required. Be sure that holes are pierced through all the balance marks so that the fabric may be marked through the holes with a marker of your choice. Place the templates on the wrong side of the fabric and mark around and transfer all balance marks.

Patches
From Fabric A
Using Template 1 mark and cut 480 patches.
Using Template 2 mark and cut 160 patches.
From Fabric B
Using Template 1 mark and cut 80 patches.
From Fabric C
Using Template 2 mark and cut 160 patches.
Using Template 3 mark and cut 80 squares 3½ x 3½ inches.
Cut 116 squares 6 x 6 inches for Prairie Point edging.

Cutting

Fabric A cut 480

Fabric A cut 160

Fabric C cut 160

Fabric C cut 80

Fabric D cut 320

Fabric E cut 40

6"

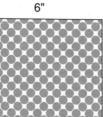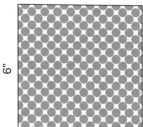
6"
Fabric C cut 116

Fabric F cut 40

Fabric B cut 80

Construction

Unit A make 80

Unit C cut 80

Unit E make 40

Unit B make 160

Unit D make 320

Unit F make 40

From Fabric D
Using Template 2 mark and cut 320 patches.
From Fabric E
Using Template 1 mark and cut 40 patches.
From Fabric F
Using Template 1 mark and cut 40 patches.

CONSTRUCTION
Piecing the pattern units
See Skill Basics section, page 69, for details on how to sew perfect curved seams.

1 Make 80 of Unit A with Fabrics A and B.
2 Make 160 of Unit B with Fabrics A and C.
3 Cut 80 of Unit C 3½-inch squares with Fabric C.
4 Make 320 of Unit D from Fabrics A and D.
5 Make 40 of Unit E from Fabrics A and E.
6 Make 40 of Unit F from Fabrics A and F.

Piecing the blocks
Four different blocks are required.
1 Make eight of Block A.

2 Make four of Block A1.

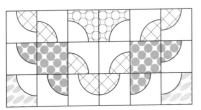

3 Make eight of Block B.

4 Make four of Block B1.

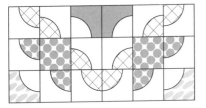

Piecing the top
See the Skill Basics section, page 70, for detailed instruction on piecing straight sets.

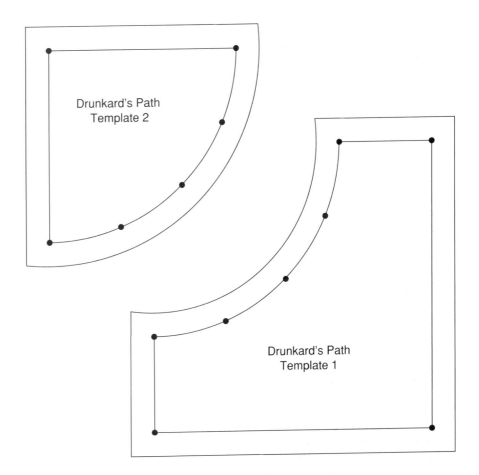

Drunkard's Path
Template 2

Drunkard's Path
Template 1

Drunkard's Path
Template 3

1 Lay out the blocks on a flat surface in the order indicated. (Refer to the colour photograph if necessary.)
2 Sew the blocks together, one row at a time.
3 Sew the rows together to complete the centre panel.

Attaching the borders
See the Skill Basics section, page 70 for help if required.
1 Attach an Inner Border A strip to either side of the centre panel.
2 Attach an Inner Border B strip to the top and bottom of the centre panel.
3 Attach a Middle Border A strip to either side of the quilt top.
4 Attach a Middle Border B strip to the top and bottom.
5 Attach an Outer Border A strip to either side of the top.
6 Attach an Outer Border B strip to the top and bottom.

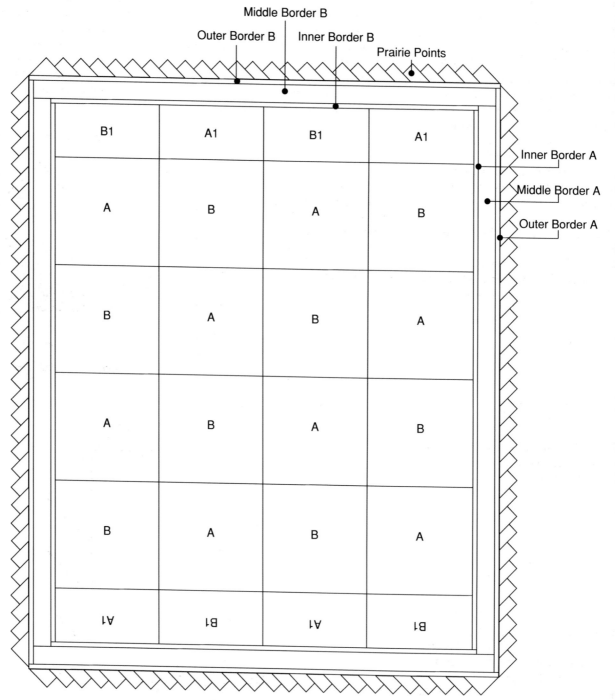

Drunkard's Path layout

Piecing the backing

Follow the method described on page 8, which avoids having a seam running down the centre of the backing.

QUILTING AND FINISHING

The quilt should be layered, basted and quilted before attaching the Prairie Point edging. See the Skill Basics section, page 72, for a detailed explanation. Simple outline quilting helps to define the mosaic-like design and you may wish to try some fancy quilting within the 3-inch border section. **Caution:** if you are using the Prairie Point edging, be sure to quilt no closer than 1 inch from the outer edge of the quilt top (this will allow the backing fabric to be folded out of the way while the Prairie Points are attached).

Making and attaching the Prairie Points

1 The Prairie Points are made from the 116 6-inch squares of Fabric C.

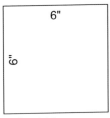

6"

6"

Cut 116 squares

2 Fold a square in half diagonally with the wrong sides together. Press the crease.

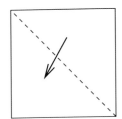

3 Fold exactly in half again, as illustrated, and press firmly. The raw edges will all lie on the long side of the folded triangles.

4 Slip the triangles one inside the

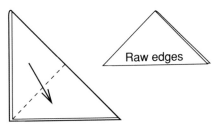

Raw edges

other to form the border edging.

5 Thirty-two Prairie Points are needed for each side of the quilt, with twenty-six each required for the top and the bottom edges. They are sewn to the quilt top and wadding, but not the backing.

Slip the triangles one inside the other so that they lie point to point along the raw edges. In the illustration one point of triangle A meets one point of triangle C.

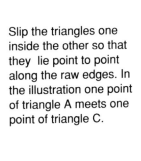

A

B

C

Starting at a corner, with the top of the layered quilt facing uppermost, and using a ¼-inch seam allowance, attach the triangles securely to the Outer Border and the wadding (fold back the backing fabric so you do not stitch through it).

6 Fold back the Prairie Points and press the seam allowance so the triangles lie flat. Turn in the quilt backing to align with the seam joining the Prairie Points to the quilt top, and slip-stitch into place to complete the quilt.

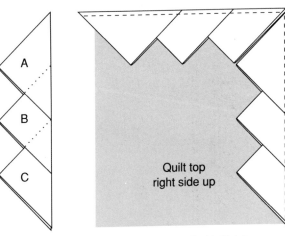

Quilt top right side up

Attaching the Prairie Points

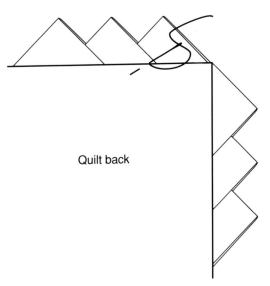

Quilt back

Slip stitching the backing fabric

PHILIPPA'S STAR

The design echoes the tiled hallways of mid-nineteenth century terraced houses and church interiors. Like all medallion quilts, construction starts at the centre and extends outwards in a series of pieced borders. Because of the many triangle shapes care needs to be taken in the placement of grain lines and handling of the bias edges.
Several set in seams are required to complete the piecing. These factors bring the making of the quilt into the intermediate category.
However, the techniques required are not difficult and detailed instructions are given in the Skill Basics section.

QUILT SIZE 65 x 85 inches

The illustrations use light, medium and dark values to define the design. Full-size templates are provided. Be sure to pierce the templates at seam junction lines so dot marks can be made at seam junction points on the wrong side of the fabric. Template 9 is a special Angle Guide for Centre Borders A and B. It will be used to mark the angles and dots for the set in seams required to attach them to the Pieced Centre Border. Read through all instructions before starting and refer to the Skill Basics section for any technical help you may require.

MATERIALS
(based on 42-inch fabric width)

Outer Border B strip

Pieced Outer Border B

Border B

Pieced Triangle Corner Panel

Pieced Triangle Corner Panel

Centre Border B

Pieced Centre Border

Centre Border A

Centre Border Br

Pieced Centre Border

Centre Border A

Centre Medallion

Centre Medallion

Star block

Medallion Triangles

Outer Border A

Pieced Outer Border A

Border A

Border A

Pieced Outer Border A

Outer Border A

Centre Border A

Pieced Centre Border

Centre Border Br

Centre Border A

Pieced Centre Border

Centre Border B

Pieced Triangle Corner Panel

Pieced Triangle Corner Panel

Border B

Pieced Outer Border B

Outer Border B

Light fabric: 2½ yards
Medium fabric: 2 yards
Dark fabric: 3½ yards
Backing fabric: 5½ yards
Wadding: 80 x 96 inches (double size)

CUTTING

From the light fabric

1 Pieced Outer Border: using Template 1 cut 16 triangles. Using Template 3 cut 96 triangles, making sure that the straight grain runs parallel to the longest side of the triangle.

2 Pieced Triangle Panel: using Template 4 cut 40 triangles making sure that the straight grain runs parallel with the shortest sides of the triangle.

3 Pieced Centre Border: using Template 5 cut 72 squares.

4 Centre Medallion: using Template 3 cut 40 triangles, making sure that the straight grain runs parallel to the shortest sides of the triangle.

5 Star Block: using Template 6 cut four triangular background patches. Reverse Template 6 to make Template 6r and cut four 6r triangle patches (mirror images of the Template 6 patches).

From the medium fabric

1 Pieced Outer Border: using Template 2 cut 52 squares.

2 Pieced Triangle Panel: using Template 4 cut 24 triangles, making sure the straight grain runs parallel with the shortest sides of the triangle.

3 Pieced Centre Border: using Template 5 cut 36 squares.

4 Centre Medallion: using Template 5 cut 24 triangles, making sure that the straight grain runs parallel with the shortest sides of the triangle.

5 Star Block: cut one 2¼-inch strip from selvedge to selvedge. Cut one 2½-inch strip from selvedge to selvedge.

From the dark fabric

Remove the selvedge and cut the border strips first (see below). In steps 1 to 4, cut the strips down the long or warp grain, parallel with the selvedge.

1 Outer Border A: cut two strips 3 x 80½ inches.

2 Outer Border B: cut two strips 3 x 65½ inches.

3 Border A: cut two strips 3 x 60½ inches.

4 Border B: cut two strips 3 x 50½ inches.

5 Centre Border A and B: cut eight strips 2¼ x 35 inches along the weft grain, from selvedge to selvedge.

6 Pieced Centre Border: using Template 1 cut 60 triangles. Using Template 5 cut 12 squares.

7 Centre Medallion: cut two squares 10⅛ x 10⅛ inches. Cut each square in half across one diagonal to yield four triangles.

8 Star Block: cut one 2¼-inch strip from selvedge to selvedge. Cut one 2½-inch strip from selvedge to selvedge.

9 Continuous French binding: cut eight 2½-inch strips from selvedge to selvedge.

CONSTRUCTION

Piecing the Star block

The Star block at the centre of the medallion has very slender points with several seam lines converging on the outer edges of the block. To maintain the sharpness of the points, a strip piecing and set in seam construction method is used. It uses the dot to dot

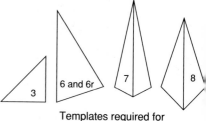

Templates required for
Centre Medallion

sewing technique described in the Skill Basics section (page 69). The illustration above shows the templates required to piece this section.

1 Reduce the stitch length on the sewing machine and sew together one medium and one dark 2¼-inch strip along the long edge. Press open the seam allowance.

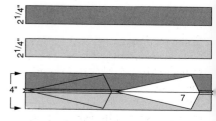

2 Using Template 7, line up the pressed seam line with the centre line on the template and mark four narrow kite-shaped patches onto the wrong side of the fabric. Mark dots at each seam junction. Cut out.

3 With a shortened stitch length on the sewing machine sew together one medium and one dark 2½-inch strip along the long edge. Press open the seam allowance.

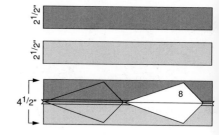

4 Using Template 8, line up the pressed seam line with the centre line on the template and mark four wide kite-shaped patches onto the

wrong side of the fabric. Mark dots at each seam junction point. Cut out.

Using the triangles cut from the light background fabric (Templates 6 and 6r), and the narrow kite-shaped patches (Template 7) make four of Unit A.

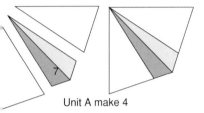

Unit A make 4

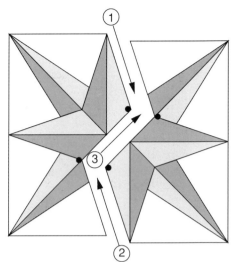

① ③ ②

Three-step seam to complete the Star block

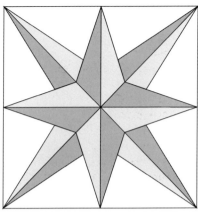

Match the dot marks and sew the seams from edge to edge. Press seams towards the background fabric.

Refer to illustration and attach a wide kite-shaped patch to Unit A to make Unit B. Make four. Finish the seam with a back stitch at the dot mark illustrated. Do not sew into the seam allowance at this point. Press seam towards background fabric.

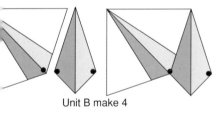

Unit B make 4

A two-step seam is required to make Unit C. Refer to the illustration.

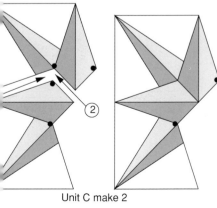

Unit C make 2

(i) Sew from the outer edge to the dot marks illustrated. Stop the seam with a back stitch at the dot marks. Do not sew into the seam allowance at this point.

(ii) Sew from the edge of the inner points to the dot marking the finish of the first step of the seam. Back stitch, taking care not to sew into the seam allowance.

Make two of Unit C. Press the first part of seam towards background fabric. Press the second part of the seam open.

8 A set in seam, consisting of three steps, is required to complete the Star block. See illustration above for sewing sequence.

(i) Sew from the outer edge to the dot marks illustrated. Stop the seam with a back stitch at the dot marks. Do not sew into the seam allowance at this point.

(ii) Sew from the remaining outer edge to the dot marks illustrated. Stop the seam with a back stitch at the dot marks. Do not sew into the seam allowance at this point.

(iii) Pin baste to match the centre seams of the star and complete the block by sewing from dot to dot across the centre of the star. Be careful to stop and start the seam at the dot marks and do not sew into the seam allowances.

Press the first and second parts of the seam towards the background

fabric. Press the third part of the centre seam open.

Piecing the Centre Medallion

1 Four dark-coloured 10⅞-inch triangles are used to frame the Star block. Attach opposite sides first. Press seam allowances away from the star.

straight grain

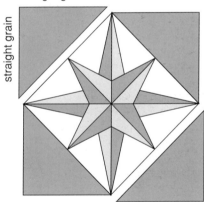

2 The triangles for Unit D are cut with Template 3 with the straight grain running parallel to the short sides of the triangle. Join the patches to make four of Unit D.

straight grain

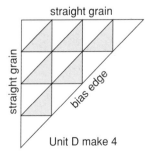

Unit D make 4

3 Complete the Medallion section by joining Unit Ds to all four sides of the framed star block. Refer to illustration and join opposite sides first.

The Centre Border section

The Pieced Centre Border consists of a stepped series of light and medium-coloured squares. The stepped design of the squares is framed with small dark-coloured triangles and border strips. Set

The Centre Medallion section

in seams will be required to fit the border neatly. The templates required for this part of the quilt are shown below. Number 9 is the Special Angle Guide that will be used to mark angles and dot marks on Centre Borders A and B.

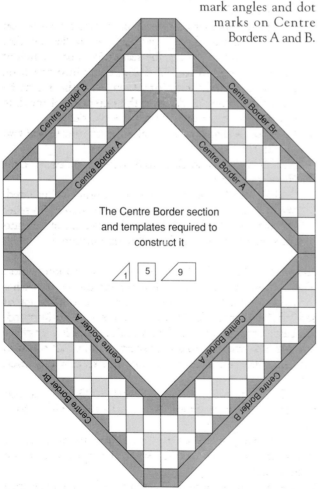

The Centre Border section and templates required to construct it

Dimensions given are mathematically correct for the border strips, but because of the bias edges you may find that some slight easing is necessary to make the section fit neatly.

Marking and cutting the border strips

The eight dark strips (2¼ x 35 inches) will be required plus the special Angle Guide (Template 9).

Cut eight strips 2¼" x 35"

Centre Border A

1 Fold the strip in half and lightly finger-press to mark its centre point. Measure 14¾ inches in each direction and mark with a pin. The pins should be 29½ inches apart. The wrong side of the fabric should be uppermost.

2 Align the point of the the Angle Guide (Template 9 and 9r) with the pins, as illustrated. Mark the angle and dot marks. Reverse the template and mark the other end. Mark and cut four Centre Border A strips.

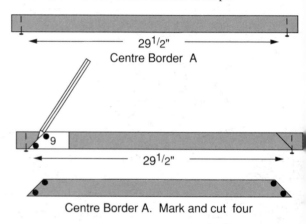

29½"
Centre Border A

29½"

Centre Border A. Mark and cut four

Centre Border B and Br

These strips are parallelograms. Br is the mirror image of B.

1 Fold the strip in half and lightly finger-press to mark its centre point. The wrong side of the fabric should be uppermost. Measure 14⅛ inches in each direction and mark with a pin. The pins should be 28¼ inches apart.

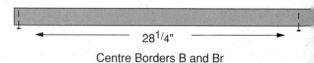

28¼"
Centre Borders B and Br

2 Using the Angle Guide (Template 9) at 90° to the edge of the strip, mark the wrong side of the fabric with a perpendicular line at each pin mark.

3 Place the Angle Guide (Template 9r) parallel with the edge of the strip, as illustrated. Using a pin, match the seam dot of the Angle Guide with the perpendicular line on the strip, keeping the edge of the guide parallel with

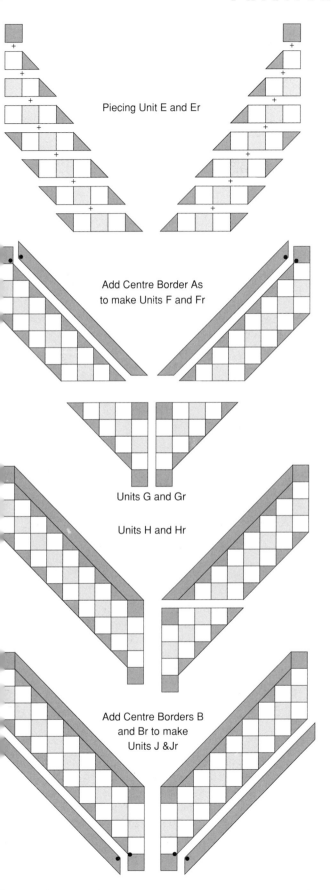

Piecing Unit E and Er

Add Centre Border As
to make Units F and Fr

Units G and Gr

Units H and Hr

Add Centre Borders B
and Br to make
Units J &Jr

the edge of the strip, and mark the 45° angle onto the strip using the two dot marks. Rotate the Angle Guide and mark the other end of the parallelogram in the same way. Cut along the angled lines. Mark and cut two of these Border B strips.

4   Place the Angle Guide (Template 9) parallel with the edge of the strip. Using a pin, match the seam dot of the Angle Guide with the perpendicular line on the strip, keeping the edge of the guide parallel with the edge of the strip, and mark the 45° angle onto the strip using the two dot marks. Rotate the Angle Guide and mark the other end of the parallelogram in the same way. Cut along the angled lines. Mark and cut two of these Border Br strips.

Piecing the Pieced Centre Border

Units E and Er are mirror images of each other. They are constructed using the small triangles and squares cut with Templates 1 and 5. Centre Borders A and B are added to complete the Centre Border section using the set in seam technique.

1   Refer to diagram top left and make two of Unit E and two of Unit Er.
2   Add Centre Border As to each unit using a two-step set in seam to make Units F and Fr. Refer to diagram. Sew the long seam first. Stop the seam with a back stitch at the dot marks illustrated. Do not sew into the seam allowances at these points. Complete the seams by sewing from the dot marks at the inner side of the dark square to the outer edge of the border section.
3   Refer to the diagrams and make two of Unit G and two of Unit Gr.
4   Attach Units G and Gr to to F and Fr make two of Unit H and two of Hr.
5   Add Centre Border B strips to each unit as illustrated, making Units J and Jr. Again use a two-step set in seam to attach the strips, making sure that you do not sew into the seam allowances at the dot marks illustrated.

Joining the Centre Border section to the Medallion section

The diagram on the next page illustrates the set in sewing sequence required to join these sections. Be careful not to sew into the seam allowances at the dot marks illustrated. Pin baste, or tack if preferred, to help fit the borders neatly.

Seam 1: Sew from dot to dot, as illustrated. Do not sew into the seam allowances. Start and stop the seam with a back stitch.

Seam 2: Sew from dot to dot, as illustrated. Do not sew into the seam allowances. Start and stop the seam with a back stitch.

Seam 3: Starting at the outer edge sew seam to the inner dot marks. Stop seam with a back stitch. Do not sew into the seam allowance.

Seam 4: Sew from dot to dot, as illustrated. Do not sew into

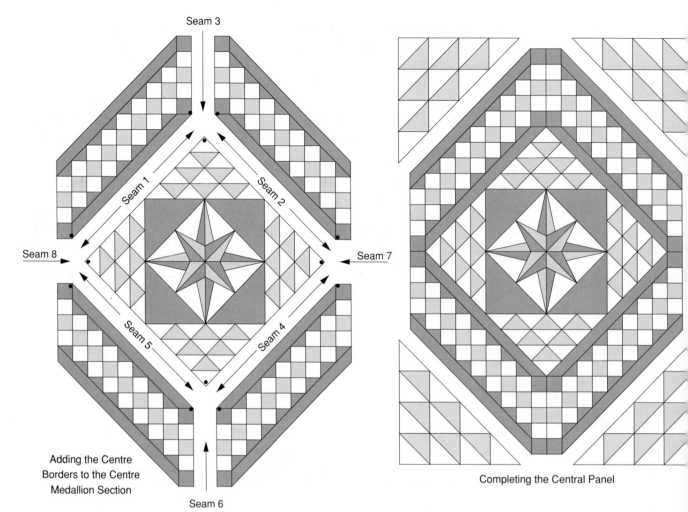

Adding the Centre
Borders to the Centre
Medallion Section

Completing the Central Panel

the seam allowances. Start and stop the seam with a back stitch.

Seam 5: Sew from dot to dot, as illustrated. Do not sew into the seam allowances. Start and stop the seam with a back stitch.

Seam 6: Starting at the outer edge sew seam to the inner dot marks. Stop seam with a back stitch. Do not sew into the seam allowance.

Seam 7: Starting at the outer edge sew seam to the inner dot marks. Stop seam with a back stitch. Do not sew into the seam allowance.

Seam 8: Starting at the outer edge sew seam to the inner dot marks. Stop seam with a back stitch. Do not sew into the seam allowance.

COMPLETING THE CENTRAL PANEL

The central panel of the quilt top is completed by the addition of four Pieced Triangle Panels (Unit K).

1 Make four Unit K, taking care not to stretch the bias edges.

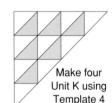

Make four Unit K using Template 4

2 Complete the central panel by attaching a Unit K to each of the outer edges of Centre Border B.

MAKING THE PIECED OUTER BORDERS

The Pieced Outer Borders are constructed using the small triangle (Template 1), large square (Template 2) and medium triangle (Template 3). Take care that medium triangle patches are cut with the grain running parallel to the longest side of the triangle. The small triangle patches should be cut with the grain running parallel to the shortest sides of Template 1.

1 Join two triangles to opposite sides of a large square patch to make Unit L. Make 48 of Unit L (see below).

Unit L. Make 48

2 Attach two small triangles and one medium triangle to a large square patch to make Unit M. See below for the sewing sequence. Make eight of Unit M.

Unit M. Make 8

Pieced Outer Border Strip B. Make 2

Join twelve Unit L and two Unit M to make Pieced Border Strip A. Make two.

Refer to diagram above. Join ten Unit L and two Unit M to make Pieced Border Strip B. Make two.

COMPLETING THE QUILT TOP

The border sections are attached section by section. The diagram on page 15 illustrates the piecing sequence. Press seams towards the dark fabric strips, throughout.

1 Attach a dark fabric Border A to either side of the quilt top.
2 Attach a dark fabric Border B to the top and bottom.
3 Attach a Pieced Outer Border A to either side of the quilt top.
4 Attach a Pieced Outer Border B to the top and bottom.
5 Attach an Outer Border A to either side of the quilt top
6 Attach an Outer Border B to the top and bottom to complete the quilt top.

PIECING THE BACKING

Follow the method on page 8, which avoids having a seam running down the centre of the backing.

QUILTING AND FINISHING

See the Skill Basics section (page 72) for notes on how to layer and baste the quilt sandwich in preparation for quilting. Advice is also given on attaching a hanging sleeve and attaching a continuous French binding.

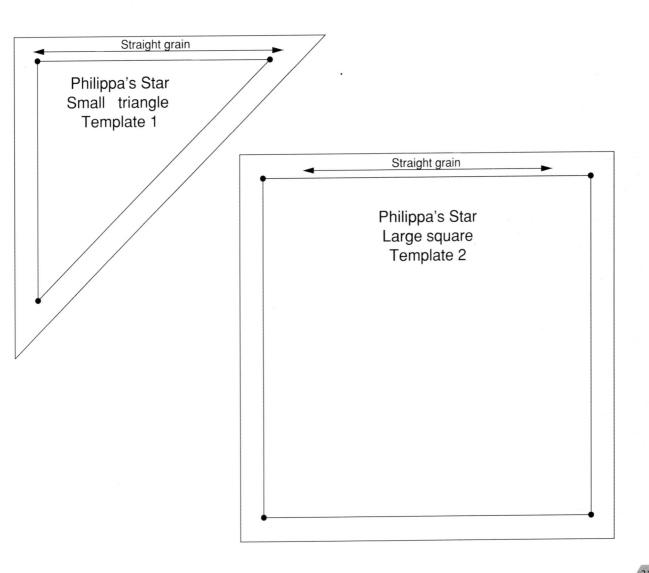

Straight grain

Philippa's Star
Small triangle
Template 1

Straight grain

Philippa's Star
Large square
Template 2

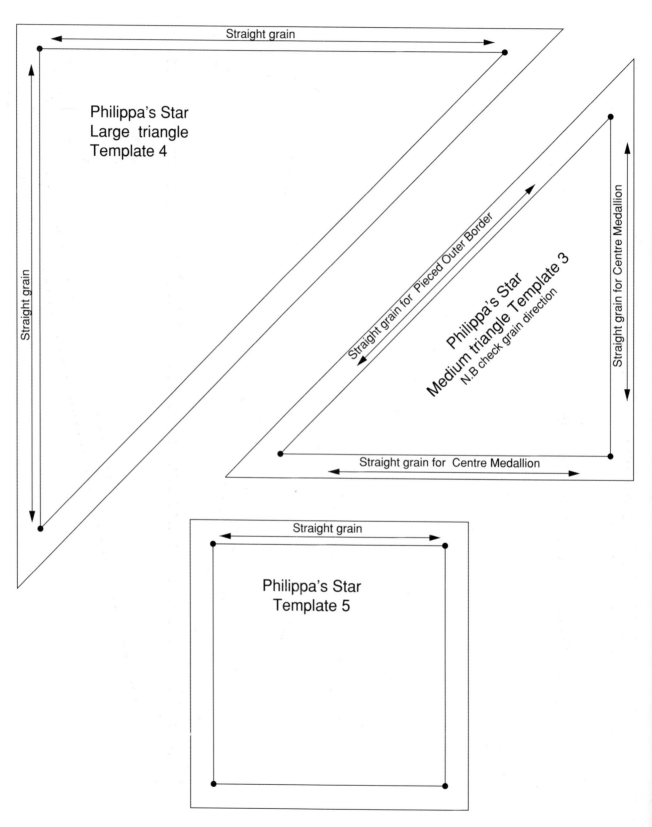

Straight grain

Philippa's Star
Large triangle
Template 4

Straight grain

Straight grain for Pieced Outer Border

Philippa's Star
Medium triangle Template 3
N.B check grain direction

Straight grain for Centre Medallion

Straight grain for Centre Medallion

Straight grain

Philippa's Star
Template 5

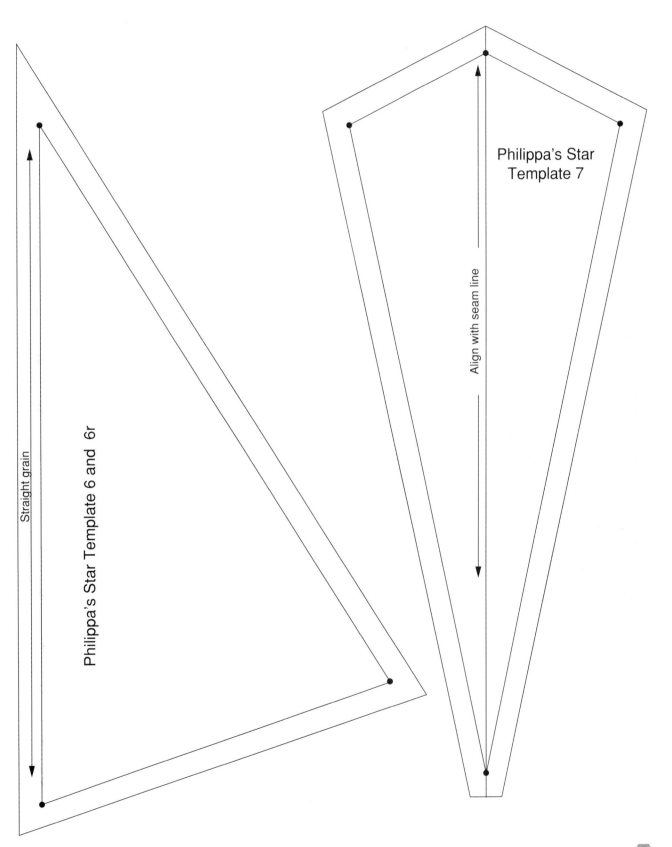

Straight grain

Philippa's Star Template 6 and 6r

Philippa's Star
Template 7

Align with seam line

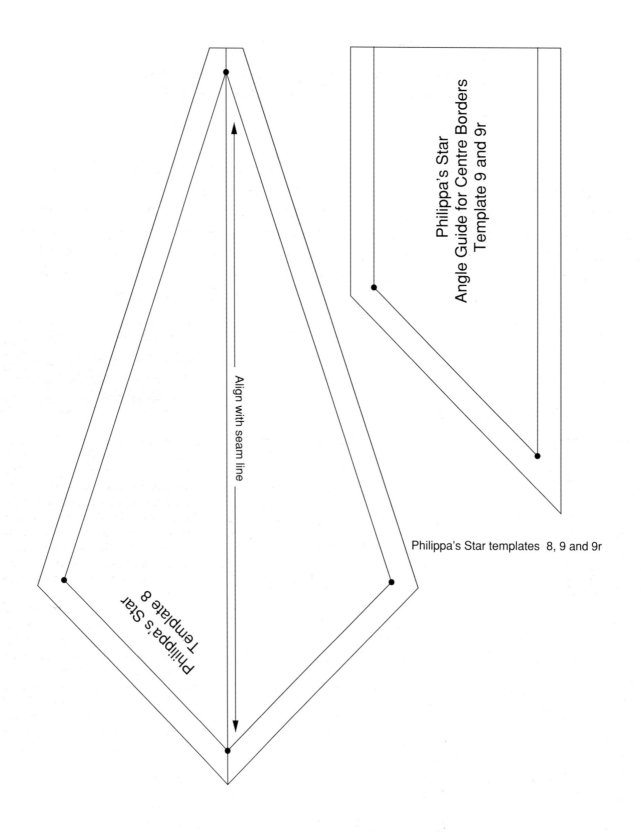

Philippa's Star
Angle Guide for Centre Borders
Template 9 and 9r

Philippa's Star templates 8, 9 and 9r

Align with seam line

Philippa's Star
Template 8

Jacob's Ladder

Design blocks and half-block units are arranged to form a rotating symmetrical setting of squares, triangles and trapeziums. The centre panel of the quilt is framed by a wide, mitred border composed of five strips. The arrangement of the blocks and border strips makes the use of just two contrasting fabrics a very easy and effective option. The design would also work well with a collection of scrap fabrics. Sort the scraps into two piles, one dark, one light. If you cannot decide whether a fabric is dark or light do not use it, as the effectiveness of the setting relies on a very strong contrast between lights and darks.

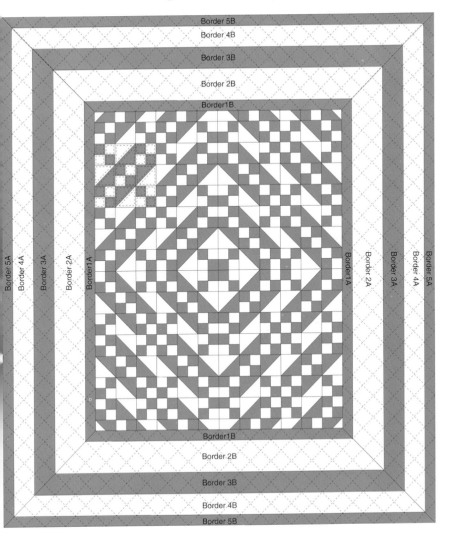

QUILT SIZE 84 x 96 inches

BLOCK SIZE 12 inches

BLOCKS REQUIRED 16 Jacob's Ladder blocks plus 4 Unit A and 4 Unit B

Instructions are given for rotary cutting and speed construction methods using the sewing machine. Except where stated, all seams use a ¼-inch seam allowance. It is important that the ¼-inch seam sewn is precisely the same as the ¼-inch seam allowance cut with your rotary cutter. See the Skill Basics section for an explanation of how to achieve this (page 68).

If you prefer a more traditional construction approach, cut the border strips first and then refer to the template cutting guide. Full-size templates are given on page 30. The size of the quilt makes it suitable for a double or queen size bed. Read through all instructions before starting and refer to the Skill Basics section for any technical help you may require.

MATERIALS

(based on 42-inch fabric width)

Light fabric: 5 yards

Dark fabric: 5¼ yards

Backing fabric: 8½ yards
Wadding: 108 x 102 inches (king size)

CUTTING

The dimensions given for the border strips include a working allowance to enable easy fitting of the mitred corners. Remove a selvedge and cut the border strips first. Cut down the length of the fabric on the long, warp grain parallel to the selvedge, and then put to one side.

From the light fabric

1 Border 2A: cut two strips 6½ x 76 inches.
2 Border 4A: cut two strips 4½ x 98 inches.
3 Border 2B: cut two strips 6½ x 68 inches.
4 Border 4B: cut two strips 4½ x 84 inches.
5 Squares: cut thirteen strips 2½ x 42 inches on the straight weft grain from selvedge to selvedge.
6 Trapeziums: cut one strip 2½ x 42 inches. Use Template 3 to mark and cut four patches. Reverse the template for mirror image Template 3r and mark and cut another four patches.
7 Small half-square triangles: cut one strip 2⅞ x 15 inches. Slice into four squares 2⅞ x 2⅞ inches. Slice the squares in half across one diagonal to produce eight half-square triangles.
8 Large half-square triangles: cut six rectangles 17 x 12 inches for fast triangles construction method.

From the dark fabric

1 Border 1a: cut two strips 2½ x 68 inches.
2 Border 1b: cut two strips 2½ x 56 inches.
3 Border 3a: cut two strips 4½ x 84 inches.
4 Border 3b: cut two strips 4½ x 76 inches.
5 Border 5a: cut two strips 2½ x 100 inches.
6 Border 5b: cut two strips 2½ x 88 inches.
7 Squares: cut thirteen strips 2½ x 42 inches.

8 Trapeziums: cut one strip 2½ x 42 inches. Use Template 3 to mark and cut four patches. Reverse the template for mirror image Template 3r and mark and cut another four patches.
9 Small half-square triangles: cut one strip 2⅞ x 15 inches. Slice into four squares 2⅞ x 2⅞ inches. Slice the squares in half across one diagonal to produce eight half-square triangles
10 Large half-square triangles: cut seven rectangles 17 x 12 inches for fast triangle construction method OR using Template 2 mark and cut eighty triangles.
11 Continuous binding: cut nine strips 2½ x 42 inches from selvedge to selvedge.

From the backing fabric

Cut one rectangle 42 x 88 inches.
Cut two rectangles 30 x 88 inches.

CONSTRUCTION

Piecing the pattern units

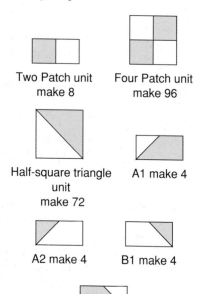

Two Patch unit
make 8

Four Patch unit
make 96

Half-square triangle unit
make 72

A1 make 4

A2 make 4

B1 make 4

B2 make 4

Strip piecing the Two Patch and Four Patch units

1 Place the 13 light and 13 dark 2½ x 42-inch strips into two piles.

Shorten the stitch length slightly on the sewing machine.

2 Place a dark strip and a light strip right sides together and sew a ¼-inch seam along the long edge. Press the seam open smoothly with a dry iron. Check that the width of the sewn strips is 4½ inches. Join each of the thirteen pairs of strips in this way.

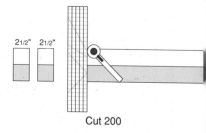

3 Using rotary cutting equipment cut 2½-inch slices to produce 200 Two Patch units.

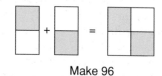

Cut 200

4 Pin baste to match the seam junctions and join the segments to make 96 Four Patch units.

$\square + \square = \square$

Make 96

Fast patch triangles for the half-square triangle units

There are many speed methods for joining triangles. This one is my favourite because it makes economical use of the fabric and is sewn using one seam only. Twelve half-square triangle units are produced.

1 Select the seven dark and seven light 17 x 12 inch-rectangles.
2 Place a light rectangle and a dark rectangle right sides together. Using a rotary ruler and fabric

marker of choice draft a 4⅞-inch grid of six squares on the wrong side of the light fabric. Draft a diagonal line through each square, as illustrated.

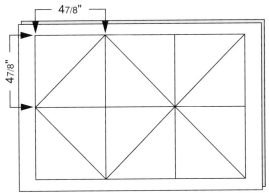

Half-square triangle grid

3 Draw a sewing line ¼ inch to either side of the diagonal lines, and pin. Take care that the positioning of the pins will not obstruct the passage of the sewing machine.

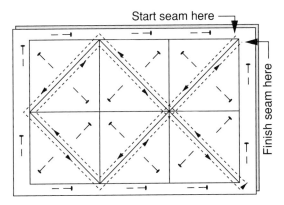

4 Study the illustration. Reduce the stitch length on the sewing machine slightly and sew on the diagonal stitching lines. By sewing off the edge of the grid and pivoting the fabric it is possible to complete the sewing of the grid with just one seam.

5 Remove all the pins and, starting at the outer edge of the grid, cut on the horizontal and vertical lines.

6 The resulting squares will each have two lines of stitching parallel to the diagonal line. Cut on the diagonal line between the two rows of stitching.

7 Open out the half-square triangle units and press open the seam allowances. Trim the 'ears' that appear, to complete the unit. Repeat to make 72 units.

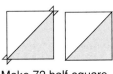

Make 72 half-square triangle units

Pattern Units A1, A2, B1 and B2
Refer to prevoius page and join the trapeziums and small triangles to make four of each unit.

Piecing the blocks
1 Lay out the Four Patch and half-square triangle units as illustrated.

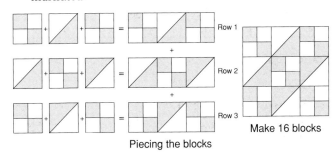

Piecing the blocks

Make 16 blocks

2 Join the units together to form Rows 1, 2 and 3. Press.
3 Join the rows together to complete the block. Press. Make sixteen blocks.

Unit A construction
1 Lay out the pattern units as illustrated.

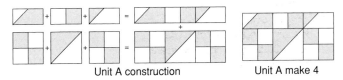

Unit A construction   Unit A make 4

2 Join the units to make the two rows.
3 Join the rows to complete the unit. Make four units.

Unit B construction
1 Lay out the pattern units as illustrated.

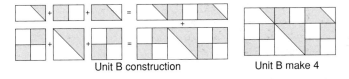

Unit B construction   Unit B make 4

2 Join the units to make the two rows.
3 Join the rows to complete the unit. Make four units.

Piecing the centre panel
1 Lay out the blocks on a large surface, as illustrated overleaf. (To avoid confusion it helps to replace the blocks into the sequence each time a seam is sewn.)
2 Starting with Row 1 sew block to block to complete each of the six rows. Replace each row into the proper sequence.
3 Join the rows to complete the panel. (See next page.)
4 Remove any loose threads and press.

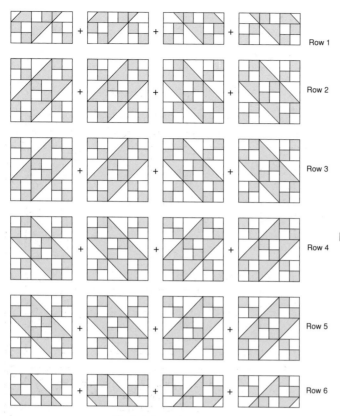

Piecing the centre panel

Piecing the border

The main colour illustration (page 25) shows that Borders A and B consist of five strips. Border A is attached to each side of the quilt, and Border B is attached to the top and bottom edges of the quilt. The dimensions of the strips vary and those given in the cutting guide include a working allowance. Construction of the border is simplified by joining the border strips together before attaching them to the quilt top. Each border section is thus treated as one piece of fabric.

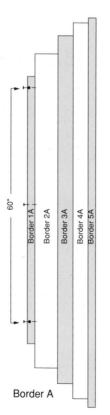

Border A

Border A

1 Five border strips, 1A, 2A, 3A, 4A and 5A, are joined together to make Border A. Fold each strip in half and finger press to mark the centre of each strip. Weave a pin in and out of each centre crease to mark the spot.
2 Match the centre creases and sew together the five strips, as illustrated.
3 From the centre pin, measure out 30 inches in each direction. Mark each

point with a dot, then weave a pin in and out. The outer pins should be 60 inches apart. Make two Border As.

Border B

1 Border B is constructed in the same manner using border strips 1B, 2B, 3B, 4B, and 5B. Fold each strip in half and finger press to mark the centre of each strip. Weave a pin in and out of each centre crease to mark the spot.

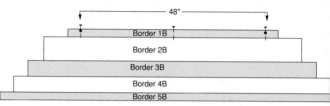

2 Match the centre creases and sew together the five strips, as illustrated.
3 From the centre pin, measure out 24 inches in each direction. Mark each point with a dot, then weave a pin in and out. The outer pins should be 48 inches apart. Make two Border Bs.

Attaching the borders

Before attaching the border strips refer to the mitred border details given in the Skill Basics (page 72) for a detailed explanation of how to check the measurements and mark the mitre. Make any adjustments required to the pin markers on the border strips.
1 Press the quilt top and mark a dot ¼ inch in from each corner, on the wrong side of the fabric.

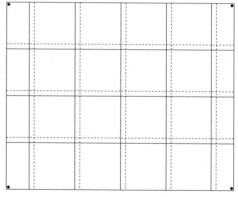

Mark dots ¼" in from each corner

2 With Border A on top, pin baste matching the dot marks and attach to one side of the quilt top using a ¼-inch seam allowance. Sew from dot to dot. Start and stop the seam with a backtack on the dot marks. Do not sew into the seam allowance at these corner points. Repeat the process until all the borders are attached.
3 Mark the mitre seam using a rotary ruler. Refer to the Skill Basics section for detailed instructions.

4 Check the mitred seam from the front and make any fine adjustments necessary to match the border stripes before sewing the seam exactly on the basting stitches. To ensure a smooth corner you may prefer to sew the seam from the front by hand using an invisible slip stitch to secure the seam.

Piecing the backing
The quilt backing consists of three rectangles. Join the rectangles together as illustrated below using a ½-inch seam allowance. Snip any selvedges to release the tension along the seam lines. Press.

QUILTING AND FINISHING
The quilt should be layered and basted in preparation for quilting. See Skill Basics section (page 72) if you need help. The main illustration shows a quilted square grid in the border areas with simple outline quilting suggested for the blocks. Alternatively a square grid could be quilted over the whole of the top. More experienced quilters could use the border areas to show off their expertise with some fancy quilting designs of their own.

See the Skill Basics section (page 74) for advice on attaching a hanging sleeve and attaching continuous French binding around the edges of the quilt.

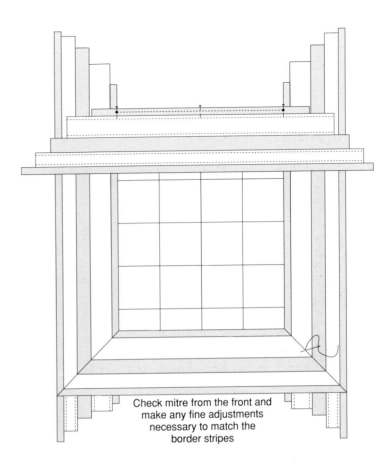

Check mitre from the front and make any fine adjustments necessary to match the border stripes

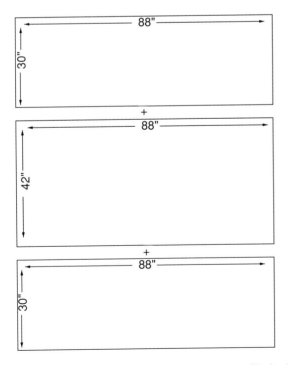
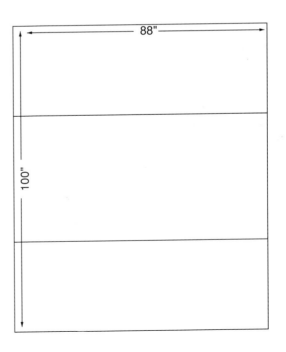

Piecing the quilt backing

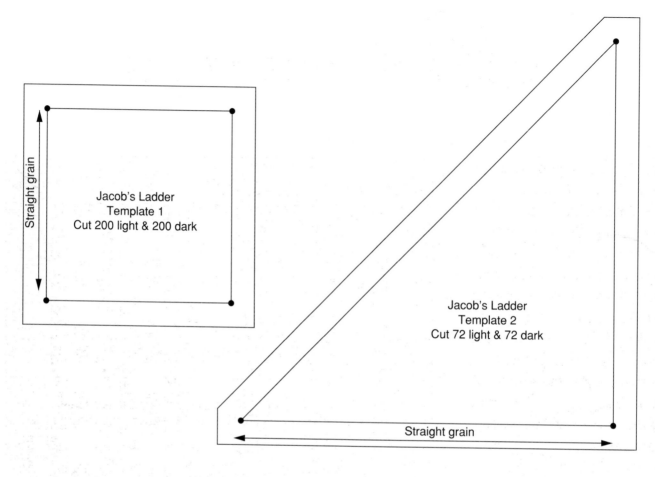

Jacob's Ladder
Template 1
Cut 200 light & 200 dark

Straight grain

Jacob's Ladder
Template 2
Cut 72 light & 72 dark

Straight grain

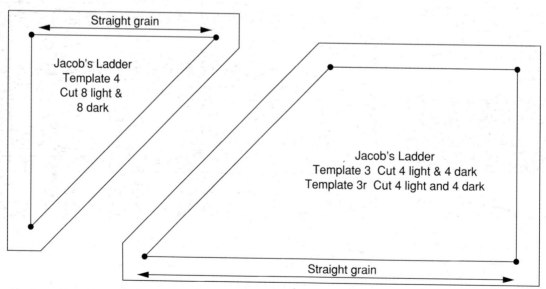

Straight grain

Jacob's Ladder
Template 4
Cut 8 light &
8 dark

Jacob's Ladder
Template 3 Cut 4 light & 4 dark
Template 3r Cut 4 light and 4 dark

Straight grain

PROVENCE STARS

Happy memories of Trets in the South of France combined with three strongly contrasting Provençal prints and a simple Star block gave this quilt its name. The same richly coloured striped border fabric is used not only for the sashing strips that outline the blocks but also to create the mitred borders that frame the quilt. The bright yellow print of the stars provides a strong contrast with the blue print used as the 'sky' fabric. The familiar Star block used is commonly known as either Evening Star or Sawtooth Star.

QUILT SIZE 65 x 85 inches
BLOCK SIZE 10 inches
BLOCKS REQUIRED 35

The pattern units making up each block consist of four small squares, one large square and four rectangular units. Each rectangular unit is constructed from one large and two smaller triangles. It is often referred to as a Wild Geese unit. The large triangle is said to represent the goose, with the two small triangles repre- senting the sky. There is more than one speed method of producing them, and the one given is my particular favourite. It avoids fiddly cutting of triangles and has the advantage of providing a bonus collection of spare half-square triangle units that can be used for another project.

The quilt can be very easily made using a combination of cotton prints using light medium and dark values as illustrated in the tonal diagram. The sashing strips and squares used in the setting are the easiest type to use. The contrast squares provide easy matching points for perfect seam matching and help to keep the top hanging straight and square. The width of the stripes in the border print determines the width of the sashing or lattice strips which separate the blocks, and also determine the width of the mitred border.

The quilt is suitable size for a single bed. It is possible (without interruptions!) to cut and piece the top in a couple of days.

Read through all instructions before starting and refer to the Skill Basics section for any technical help you may require.

For those who prefer a more relaxed traditional approach, full-size templates are on pages 34-35 Cut the border strips first and then refer to the template cutting guide.

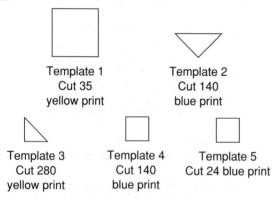

Template 1
Cut 35
yellow print

Template 2
Cut 140
blue print

Template 3
Cut 280
yellow print

Template 4
Cut 140
blue print

Template 5
Cut 24 blue print

MATERIALS

(based on 42-inch fabric width)

Border fabric: 3 yards (for striped fabric, this quantity assumes that there are sufficient repeats across the width of the fabric. It is wise to check the repeats *before* purchase)

Dark fabric (blue print): 3 yards
Light fabric (yellow print): 2¾ yards
Binding fabric: ¾ yard
Backing fabric: 6 yards
Wadding: 80 x 96 inches (double size)

CUTTING

Instructions are given for rotary cutting. (*Where applicable, cutting instructions for the traditional approach are given in italics.*) The dimensions given for the borders include a working allowance to enable easy fitting of the mitred corners. Remove a selvedge and cut the borders first.

From the border fabric (both methods)
1   Border A: cut two strips 6½ x 95 inches.
2   Border B: cut two strips 6½ x 72 inches.
3   Sashing strips: cut 58 strips 2 x 10½ inches.

From the dark fabric
1   Star block: cut 20 strips 3 x 42 inches. Slice into 140 squares 3 x 3 inches (*use Template 4 to mark and cut 140 squares*).
2   Star block: cut 20 strips 3 x 42 inches. Slice into 140 rectangles 3 x 5½ inches (*use Template 2 to mark and cut 140 triangles*).
3   Sashing squares: cut two strips 2 x 42 inches. Slice into 24 squares 2 x 2 inches (*use Template 5 to mark and cut 24 squares*).

From the light fabric
1   Star block: cut five strips 5½ x 42 inches. Slice into 35 squares 5½ x 5½ inches (*use Template 1 to mark and cut 35 squares*).
2   Star block: cut 20 strips 3 x 42 inches. Slice into 280 squares 3 x 3 inches (*use Template 3 to mark and cut 280 triangles*).

From the binding fabric (both methods)
Cut nine strips 2½ x 42 inches.

From the backing fabric (both methods)
Cut in half to make two rectangles.

CONSTRUCTION

Piecing the Star blocks
Each block consists of one large centre square surrounded by four small squares and four rectangular pattern units, commonly known as Wild Geese units. The units consist of one large and two small triangle patches. In the no-template method described below the units are easily constructed using rotary-cut rectangles and squares. **Note:** the scale of the diagrams is enlarged for clarity.

The Wild Geese units
1   On the wrong side of each 3-inch light-coloured square lightly mark a precise diagonal line from corner to corner with a fabric marker of your choice. An HB pencil is most popular for this, but may not be suitable for your fabric. See Skill Basics section (page 67) for advice on fabric markers.
2   Mark a second line ½ inch to one side of the diagonal.
3   Place a marked light-coloured square onto a dark-coloured 3 x 5½-inch rectangle, right sides together. Check

Completing the blocks

1 Lay out the patches for each block as illustrated.
2 Piece together a row at a time.
3 Join the rows to complete the block. Make 35.

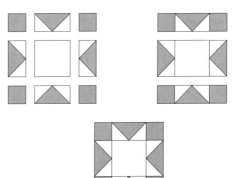

Make 35 star blocks

Attaching the sashing

1 Join a sashing strip to one side of a block as illustrated to make Unit B. Make 28.

Attach sashing strip to make Unit B

2 Refer to the diagram and join four Unit Bs side by side, plus one Star block, to form a row. Make seven rows.

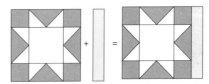

Join to make one row. Make 7 rows

3 Join five sashing strips and four sashing squares to make one long sashing strip. Make six strips.

Join sashing squares to strips to make long sashing strip.
Make 6 long strips

4 Lay out the completed rows and sashing strips as illustrated overleaf.
5 Join the strips and rows to make two large panels as illustrated overleaf. Join the panels to complete the quilt top.
6 Remove any loose threads and press.

Attaching the borders

See Skill Basics, page 72, for instructions on how to fit, mark and sew mitred borders.

that the marked lines are positioned as illustrated. Shorten the stitch length on the machine slightly and sew two seams exactly on the marked lines.

Cut between the seams and remove the bonus half square triangle unit produced. Put it to one side for a future project. Fold back the large triangle and press with a dry iron.

Place a second marked square on the opposite side of the rectangle. Check to make sure that the marked seam lines are positioned as illustrated.

Sew two seams on the marked lines. Cut between the seams to remove the spare triangle unit.

Fold back the large triangle to complete Unit A. Make 140.

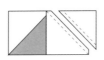

Make 140
Wild Geese units

Piecing the backing

Follow the method on page 8, which avoids having a seam running down the centre of the backing.

QUILTING AND FINISHING

See the Skill Basics section, page 72, for notes on how to layer and baste the quilt sandwich in preparation for quilting. Simple straight line or outline quilting helps to define the star pattern. Advi is also given in Skill Basics (page 74) attaching a hanging sleeve and applyi continuous French binding.

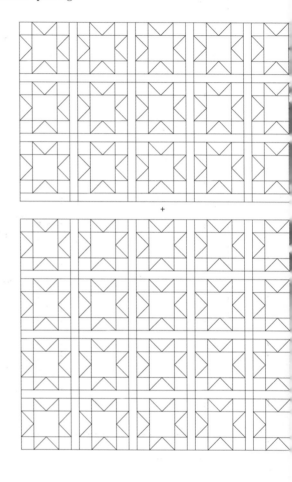

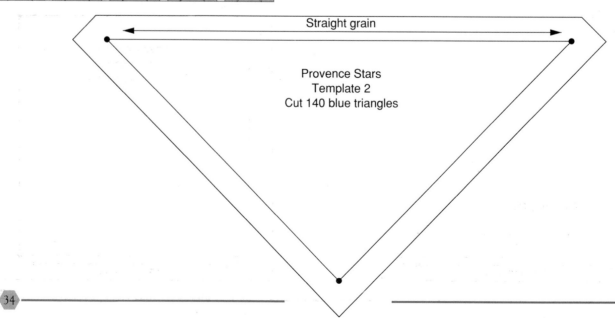

Straight grain

Provence Stars
Template 2
Cut 140 blue triangles

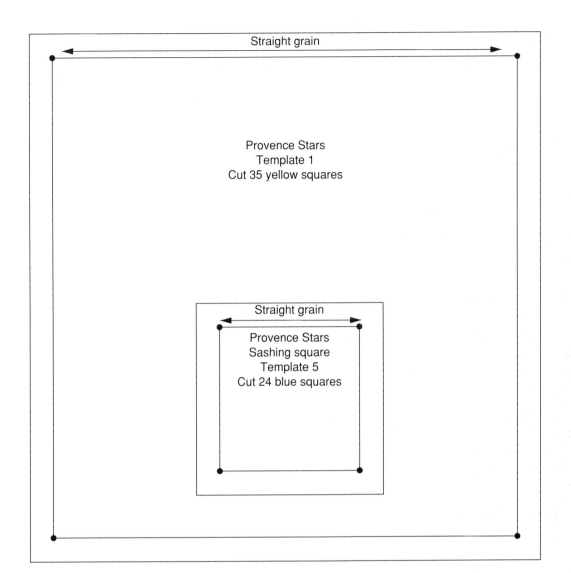

Straight grain

Provence Stars
Template 1
Cut 35 yellow squares

Straight grain

Provence Stars
Sashing square
Template 5
Cut 24 blue squares

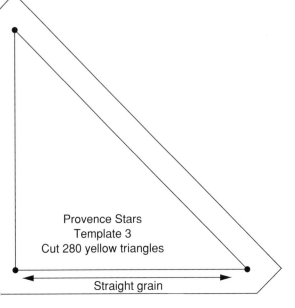

Provence Stars
Template 3
Cut 280 yellow triangles

Straight grain

Provence Stars
Template 4
Cut 140 blue squares

Straight grain

$\mathcal{B}$RIDAL WREATH

Hearts (the symbol of true love) and circles (the symbol of eternity) were often combined with leaves to create decorative garlands. Such quilts were made to celebrate the engagement or wedding of a young couple. Simple shapes are appliquéd around circles made from bias binding. The mitred border sports a series of swags also created from bias strips and is decorated at regular intervals with flamboyant red bows. A dimensional illusion is created in the bows by using the reverse side of the red print for the bow knot and loops. A classical colour scheme of bright reds and greens against a cream or white background is used.

QUILT SIZE 72 x 90 inches
BLOCK SIZE 18 inches
BLOCKS REQUIRED 12

Those with little leisure will find that the use of a hot iron together with a paper-backed fusible web such as Bondaweb will make speedy work of applying the wreaths, hearts and leaves to the background fabric. The edges of the shapes are secured with either a narrow zig-zag, blind hem stitch, or satin stitch using the sewing machine. Some may prefer the traditional method of appliqué also described which will leave the surface soft and pliable. Others may find the a mixture of contemporary and tradtional techniques works best for them

ead through all the instructions and
ake up a sample block to decide
hich method you prefer.

A quarter-circle pattern is
cluded to make creating the circle a
mple matter. There is also a posi-
oning pattern for the border swags.
ll sized patterns for all the design
ements are on pages 40 and 41. See
kill Basics Section, page 67, for infor-
ation on how to make templates.

MATERIALS
ased on 42-inch fabric width)
ight background material: 6⅝ yards
ncludes ⅝ yard for quilt binding)
reen print: 1 yard
ed print: 2¼ yards
-inch bias binding: 32¼ yards*
aper-backed fusible bonding web
uch as Bondaweb, generally sold as
andard 45 cm wide): 7¼ yards
acking fabric: 5¼ yards
adding: 80 x 96 inches (double size)

Note: bias binding can either be
urchased or you can make your own.
½-inch bias binding maker is avail-
le from suppliers listed on page 79.
sing the continuous bias binding
ethod in the Skill Basics section,
ge 75, you will require two 27-inch
uares cut into 1-inch wide strips.

ABRIC PREPARATION
re-wash (separately) all fabrics for
is project to ensure that the dyes,
pecially the red, are stable and do
t run. Washing is likely to make the
bric soft and floppy, so stabilise it
ith plenty of spray starch to restore a
isp surface. Press to smooth the
rface and eliminate any creasing.

CUTTING
emove the selvedge and cut the
order strips first. Cut along the warp
ain parallel to the selvedge and then
it to one side. Measurements given
clude a working allowance to enable
asy fitting of the mitred corners.
nless stated otherwise strips are
nerally cut on the weft grain from
lvedge to selvedge.

From the background fabric
1 Border A: cut two strips 9½ x 94
 inches parallel to the selvedge.
2 Border B: cut two strips 9½ x 76
 inches parallel to the selvedge.
3 Blocks: cut twelve squares 18½ x
 18½ inches.
4 Quilt binding: cut nine strips 2½ x
 42 inches.

From the green print
Leaves and hearts: cut nine strips 4 x
42 inches to use with 3½ x 18-inch
strips of the fusible web.

From the red print
1 Hearts: cut eight strips 4 x 42
 inches to use with 3½ x 18-inch
 strips of the fusible web.
2 Bows: cut six strips 4 x 42 inches
 to use with 3½ x 18-inch strips of
 the fusible web.

From the paper-backed fusible web
If over-handled the web of glue will
detach itself from its paper backing.
Because of this it is wisest to cut one
strip at a time across the width of the
paper before fusing it to the wrong
side of the appropriate fabric strip.

PREPARING THE BLOCKS
Registration guides
Fold each block in half and then into
quarters, and press lightly. Baste along
the creases to thread-mark the folds.
Then crease each block in half across
each diagonal. Press and again tack
along the creases to thread-mark the
folds. The thread-marks will create
registration guides that will help to
place the patches accurately.

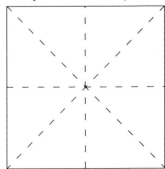
Thread marking the registration guides

The inner circle guide
Refer to the diagram and align
Template 1 on the registration guides,
as illustrated. Using a fabric marker of

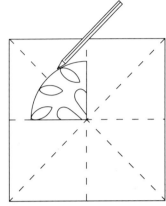
Marking the inner circle using Template 1

your choice lightly mark a quarter-
circle around the edge of the template.
Rotate the template and continue
marking until the whole circle is
marked onto the surface of the block.
Prepare all twelve blocks in this way.

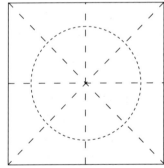
The inner circle guide

CONSTRUCTION
Machine appliqué guidelines
1 To obtain the best results from
 your sewing machine **always**
 provide some extra support
 beneath the fabric being sewn.
 Commercial stabilisers, which
 look like interlining, are used to
 prevent the fabric from stretching
 or puckering. They are easily torn
 away from the back of the work
 after the stitching is completed. I
 have found that cartridge paper
 works just as well, though extra
 care needs to be taken when
 tearing it away from the back.

Support the seam firmly with your finger and thumb and peel away the paper gently with the other hand to avoid stretching the seam. Plastic-coated papers, such as American freezer paper, can be ironed onto the wrong side of the fabric and also provide excellent support .

2   Increase the bobbin tension slightly. (In Bernina machines this is easily achieved by inserting the thread through the hole at the end of the thread-arm of the bobbin case. For other machines, turn the screw on the tension clip very slightly to the right.)

3   Decrease the top tension slightly, so that the bobbin thread will not show on the right side of the fabric being sewn.

4   Use a new needle of the correct size for the sewing thread you are using. Check in your sewing machine manual for guidance.

5   Match the upper thread to the colour of the patch being applied. If using an invisible thread be sure to use it as the upper thread only. Purchase only a very fine monofilament .004 gauge thread. It is available in either clear for light colours or smoke for darker hues. It is wise to use a pressing cloth for any appliqué work when pressing the right side. Whenever possible press the work face down onto a towel.

6   Because the bobbin thread does not show, many experienced sewers use an ecru or toning bobbin thread to conserve their coloured threads.

7   Every machine is different and will require a different adjustment depending on the type of stitch, thread and fabrics being used. The most commonly used stitches used for machine appliqué are a narrow zig-zag stitch, a satin stitch, an invisible hem stitch and the plain straight stitch. The table below lists the approximate width and length settings I most often use on my machine when working with craft cottons. Use them as a starting point for getting to know your own machine. Experiment on some scrap fabric, stabilised with spray starch, to check the width and tension of the stitch you plan to use. As soon as you obtain a satisfactory stitch write onto your sample the settings that produced the stitch and keep the sample as a reference. This will avoid having to experiment every time you sit down at the machine.

Machine setting guide for appliqué stitches

Stitch type	Approx width	Approx length
Narrow zig-zag	2	1
Satin	2½	Just under ½
Invisible hem	Just under 1	Just under 1
Straight	n/a	2-2½

Applying the wreath

The marked circle on the block is the inner edge of the wreath. Ease into and baste the inner edge of the bias binding on to the circle so it just covers the marked line. If necessary baste the outer edge also, stretching it slightly so that it lies flat on the surface. The binding can be secured to the background either by using invisible thread and the invisible hem stitch or by using a stitch of your choice. At the join, fold each end of the bias onto the straight grain, match the folds, and carefully slipstitch together. Press face down onto a towel.

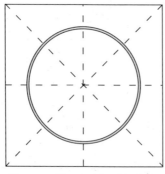

Ease and baste bias binding to the circle

Using the fusible web for design motifs

Marking the shapes onto the smooth paper side of the fusible web

The paper-backed web has a smooth side and a rough grainy side. The rough side is the web formed of glue that fuses the fabric. The smooth side is the paper backing to the web. Mark the shapes required onto the smooth paper side of the fusible web.

Place the rough side of the web down onto the wrong side of the fabric. Double-check that the smooth paper side is uppermost! Then fuse the web to the wrong side of the fabric using a hot dry iron. Leave to cool for a few minutes and then cut out the

shapes taking care to maintain the smooth curves of the shapes.

Each block requires: 16 green leaves, 14 red leaves, 6 red hearts, green hearts.

Refer to the illustration and use the registration guides to assist in the positioning of the shapes. Peel away the paper backing from the patches and place them web-side down on

e right side of the block. Fuse to the ock with a hot iron and a slightly mpened cloth.

Secure the motifs to the background using either a narrow zig-zag or stitch of your choice.

traditional paper template method
his method avoids the inevitable iffening of the quilt surface that curs when using a fusible web. The tches can be attached to the quilt ther by hand or by machine.

Using the heart template, mark and cut out sufficient cartridge paper patterns.

Lay the template down on the wrong side of the fabric and draw all round it with a fabric marker of your choice. Leave at least ½ inch between the shapes. Appliqué templates do not include a seam allowance, so it has to be added to each patch (the marked line will be the fold line of the patch, so cut out each patch about ⅜-inch outside the marked line).

Centre a paper pattern on the wrong side of the fabric.

Baste the fabric to the paper, making sure that the knot of the basting thread is on the right side of the motif. Gently gather the curved sides to form a smooth edge. Snip the seam allowance into the

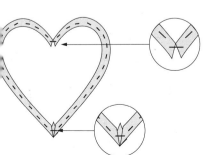

sharp inner curve and mitre the fabric at the sharp outer curve as illustrated. Press.

5 Pin the motifs into position on the block and attach them using a narrow zig-zag stitch or a stitch of your choice. Remove the basting thread.

6 From the wrong side of the block, and behind the patch, cut a small slit into the background fabric only. Remove the paper through the slit with the help of some eyebrow tweezers. Press.

Completing the top

1 Refer to the main illustration on page 36 and join the blocks first into rows. Then sew the rows together to form the central panel of the quilt.

2 Attach and mitre the borders. See Skill Basics section (page 72) for detailed guidance.

3 Using Template 4 mark placement lines for the swags along the edges of the border. The centre point of

the inner edge of the inner swag is 4 inches from the border seam.

4 Make the swags by barely covering the marked lines with the inner edge of the bias binding strips. Baste first and then secure the binding using invisible thread and the invisible hem stitch or a stitch of your choice.

Adding the bows

To create an illusion of depth, reverse the bow fabric for the loops and knot patches.

1 Mark the shapes required onto the smooth paper side of the fusible web using Templates 5, 6, 6r and 7.

2 Fuse Shape 5 to the wrong side of the bow fabric using a hot iron. Cut out.

3 Fuse Shape 6, 6r and 7 to the right side of the bow fabric using a hot iron. Cut out.

4 Peel off the backing paper and position Shape 5 onto the border and fuse in place using a damp cloth and hot iron.

5 Peel off the backing paper and position Shapes 6 and 6r and fuse in place using a damp cloth and hot iron.

6 Peel off the backing paper and position Shape 7 and fuse in place using a damp cloth and hot iron.

7 Attach to the background using a narrow zig-zag or stitch of your choice.

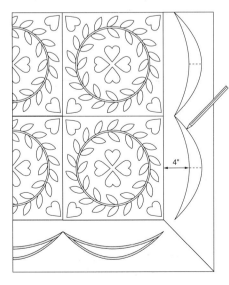

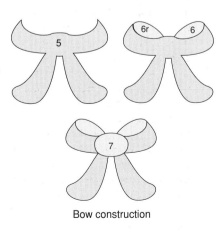

Bow construction

Piecing the backing
Follow the method on page 8, which avoids having a seam
running down the centre of the backing.

QUILTING AND FINISHING

See the Skill Basics section (page 72) for notes on how to
layer and baste the quilt sandwich. Simple outline quilting
around the motifs together with a simple filler design in the
border is all that is required to set off the design. Advice is
also given in the Skill Basics section (page 72) on attaching
a hanging sleeve and applying a continuous French binding
around the edges.

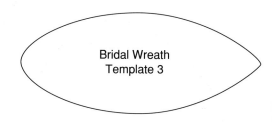

Bridal Wreath
Template 3

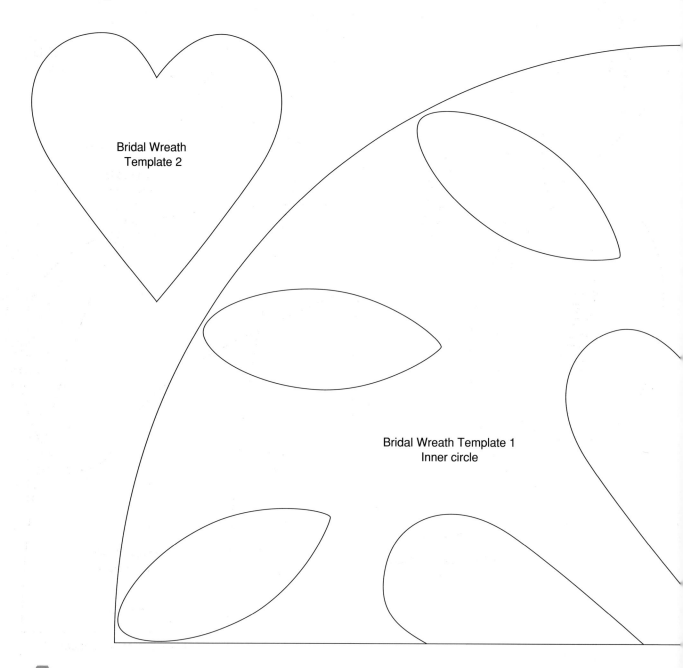

Bridal Wreath
Template 2

Bridal Wreath Template 1
Inner circle

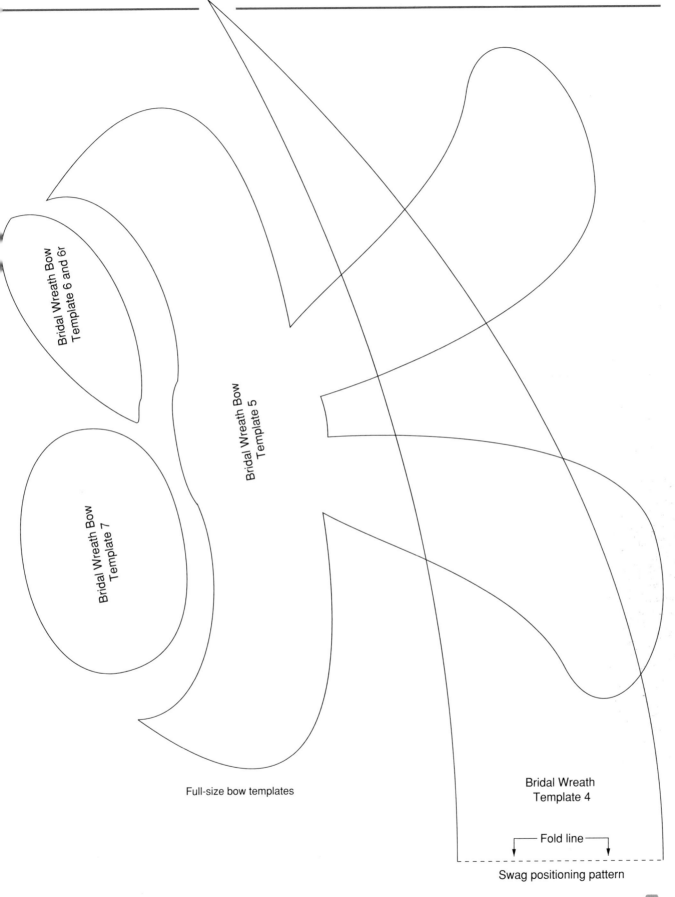

Bridal Wreath Bow
Template 6 and 6r

Bridal Wreath Bow
Template 7

Bridal Wreath Bow
Template 5

Full-size bow templates

Bridal Wreath
Template 4

├─ Fold line ─┤

Swag positioning pattern

*B*EAR'S PAW

This is a very simple design that is suitable for a beginner. Five blocks are arranged in six rows and are separated by short sashing strips with small squares. The sashing strips and squares echo the pattern units in the centre of the blocks and form a grid across the surface of the quilt. It is worth experimenting to discover different ways of using colour. By shading the sashing strips it is possible to create the illusion of a woven grid. You could also vary the colour of the blocks and use up a collection of scrap fabrics to add variety to the surface. Photocopy the line drawing given (on page 48) and experiment with coloured pencils or felt tipped pens to create your own interpretation.

QUILT SIZE 82 x 98 inches
BLOCK SIZE 14 inches
BLOCKS REQUIRED 30

Instructions are given for rotary cutting and machine piecing. For making the triangle units a speed construction method is given, which provides the right number of half-square triangle units required for each block. For those who prefer a more traditional approach, full-size templates are provided. Read through all the instructions before starting.

MATERIALS
(based on 42-inch fabric width)
Light fabric: 4¾ yards
Medium fabric: 2 yards
Dark fabric: 3 yards
Backing: 6 yards
French binding: ¾ yard
Wadding: 86 x 108 inches (queen size)

CUTTING
From the light fabric
1   Cut 37 strips 2½ inches wide. Slice into 218 rectangles measuring 2½ x 6½ inches.

2 Cut 8 strips 2½ inches wide. Slice into 120 squares measuring 2½ x 2½ inches.

3 EITHER cut 18 strips 2⅞ inches wide. Slice into 240 squares measuring 2⅞ x 2⅞ inches. Slice each square in half across one diagonal to yield 480 half square triangles. OR, if you wish to use the easy speed piecing method described below, cut 30 rectangles measuring 7 x 13 inches.

From the medium fabric
Cut 14 strips 4½ inches wide. Slice into 120 squares measuring 4½ x 4½ inches.

From the dark fabric
Remove the selvedge and cut border strips first along the warp grain parallel to the selvedge. Note: the border strip dimensions include a working allowance to ensure a good fit.

1 Border A: cut two strips 2½ x 98 inches.

2 Border B: cut two strips 2½ x 86 inches.

3 Cut the remaining strips on the weft grain at right angles to the selvedge edge. After cutting the border strips, the remaining fabric should be approximately 32 inches wide.

4 Cut nine strips 2½ inches wide. Slice into 99 squares measuring 2½ x 2½ inches.

5 EITHER cut 22 strips 2⅞ inches wide. Slice into 240 squares measuring 2⅞ x 2⅞ inches. Slice each square in half across one diagonal to yield 480 half square triangles. OR, for the easy speed piecing method described below, cut 30 rectangles measuring 7 x 13 inches.

From the backing fabric
1 Cut one rectangle 42 x 98 inches.

2 Cut two rectangles 22 x 98 inches.

CONSTRUCTION
Piecing the pattern units

The sashing strips
Join two light-coloured rectangles and one dark square to make 79 sashing strips.

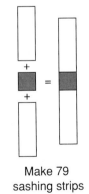

Make 79
sashing strips

Speed piecing the half-square triangle units
Each block requires sixteen units making a total of 480 units for the whole quilt. The method used is essentially the same as the one described in the Skill Basics section, page 76. A slightly different grid however is used here and two seams rather than one are required to create a group of sixteen half-square triangle units.

Make 480
half-square
triangle units

1 Select the 30 light and 30 dark 7 x 13-inch rectangles.

2 Take one of the light-fabric rectangles and, using a rotary ruler and fabric marker of choice, draft a 2⅞-inch grid of two squares by four squares onto its wrong side. Draw a diagonal line through each square, as below. Draw sewing lines ¼-inch to either side of the diagonal lines.

3 Place the marked light rectangle right sides together with a dark rectangle, and pin. Take care that the positioning of the pins will not obstruct the passage of the sewing machine.

4 Study the illustration. Reduce the stitch length slightly on the machine and sew seam 1 on the diagonal stitching lines. Follow the arrow and sew off the edge of the grid to pivot the fabric when the arrows change direction. Sew seam 2 in the same manner.

5 Remove all the pins and, starting at the outer edge of the grid, cut on the horizontal and vertical lines.

6 The resulting squares will each have two lines of stitching parallel to the diagonal line. Cut on the diagonal line between the two rows of stitching.

7 Open out the half-square triangle units and press the seam allowances open. Trim the 'ears' that appear to complete the unit. Make 480 units.

8 Join two half-square triangle units to make Unit A. Make 240.

Make
240
Unit A

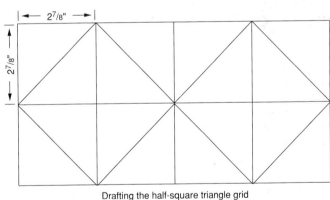

Drafting the half-square triangle grid

Start and finish seam 1 here

Start and finish seam 2 here

Bear's Paw half-square triangle grid

9 Join a light-coloured square to Unit A to make Unit B. Make 120.

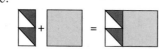
Make 120 Unit B

10 Join a medium-coloured square to Unit A to make Unit C. Make 120.

11 Join Unit B to Unit C to make Unit D. Make 120.

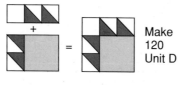
Make 120 Unit C

12 Sew a Unit D to either side of a light-coloured rectangle to make Unit E. Make 60.

Make 120 Unit D

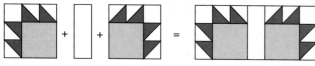
Make 60 Unit E

Piecing the block

Arrange the pattern units as illustrated, and join to complete the block. Make 30.

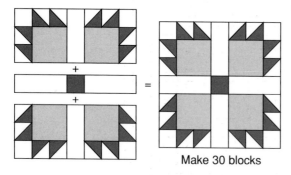
Make 30 blocks

Piecing the quilt top

1 Join a sashing strip to the side of a block, as illustrated top right. Make 24. (You will be left with six blocks which do not have a sashing strip attached.)

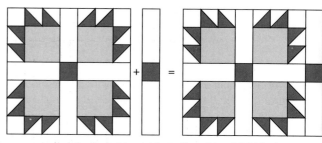
Join a sashing strip to the side of 24 blocks

2 Refer to the diagram below. Notice that the block at the right end of the row does not have a sashing strip. Join the blocks to make a row. Make six rows.

3 Join four dark squares to five short sashing strips as illustrated at the bottom of the page to make one long sashing strip. Make five of these strips.

4 Refer to the diagram on the opposite page. Lay out the rows of blocks and sashing strips as illustrated. Join together a row at a time.

Attaching the borders

Before attaching the border strips refer to the Skill Basics section, page 70, for a detailed explanation of how to check measurements and fit the border strips to the quilt top. Fit the borders. Trim and tidy any straggly threads. Press.

Piecing the backing (see opposite page below)

The backing consists of three rectangles. Join the rectangles together, as illustrated, using a ½-inch seam allowance. Snip any selvedge edges to release the tension along the seam lines. Press.

QUILTING AND FINISHING

The quilt should be layered and basted in preparation for quilting. See Skill Basics section, page 72, if you need help. A suggested quilting design is given in on page 46 and full-size quilting patterns are provided.

See the Skill Basics section, page 74, for advice on attaching a hanging sleeve and attaching continuous French binding around the edges of the quilt.

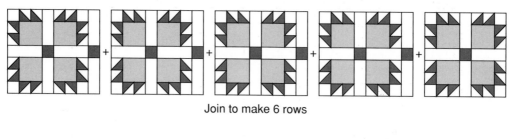
Join to make 6 rows

Make 5 long sashing strips

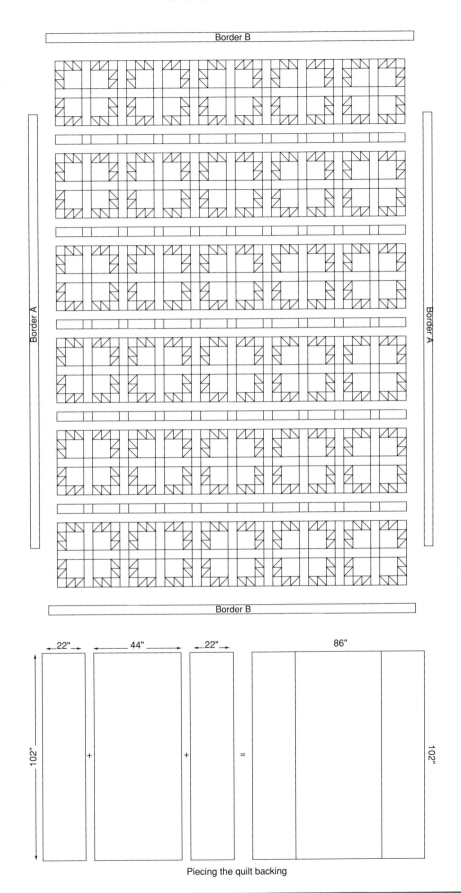

Border B

Border A

Border A

Border B

22"   44"   22"   86"

102"   +   +   =   102"

Piecing the quilt backing

Suggested quilting design

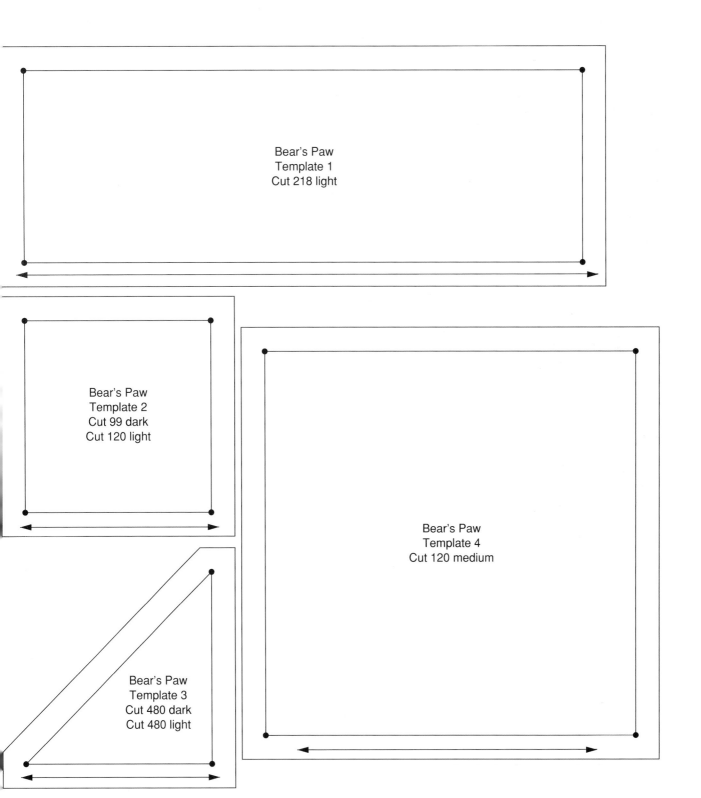

Bear's Paw
Template 1
Cut 218 light

Bear's Paw
Template 2
Cut 99 dark
Cut 120 light

Bear's Paw
Template 4
Cut 120 medium

Bear's Paw
Template 3
Cut 480 dark
Cut 480 light

Photocopy this drawing and experiment with your own colours

DOUBLE IRISH CHAIN

Double Irish Chain is one of the easiest quilts to make. Block A consists of an ordered arrangement of light, medium and dark-coloured squares. Block B is light-coloured with a medium-coloured square set in each corner. To create the symmetrical surface design an uneven number of blocks are arranged alternately in an uneven number of rows. Here five blocks are arranged side by side in seven rows. The central panel of the quilt is surrounded by a series of straight-cut border strips. Instructions are given for rotary cutting and a strip-piecing method that will make speedy work of piecing the blocks. For those who prefer to use more traditional construction methods, full-size templates are provided.

QUILT SIZE 74 x 94 inches

BLOCK SIZE 10 inches

BLOCKS REQUIRED 18 Block A and 17 Block B

Double Irish Chain

The design creates a splendid canvas on which to practise and display fine quilting skills. The illustration shows diagonal quilting lines passing through the centre of each small square. A three-stranded Celtic knot-work motif is repeated in the open block areas and a simple interlaced design creates a handsome border. A full-scale pattern is provided for the motif, together with a half-scale border pattern, see pages 52 and 53. For clarity, read through all the instructions before starting.

MATERIALS

(based on 42-inch fabric width)
The yardage given is based on the use of the rotary cutter and a strip piecing construction method together with the use of just three contrasting coloured fabrics.

Light fabric: 3¾ yards
Medium fabric: 2 yards
Dark fabric: 3¼ yards (includes yardage for binding)
Backing fabric: 5¾ yards
Wadding: 86 x 108 inches (queen size)

CUTTING

Remove the selvedge and cut the border strips first on the warp or long grain, parallel to the selvedge of the fabric. The measurements given for the border strips include a working allowance to enable easy fitting of the borders. Once the borders have been cut all the remaining strips are cut on the weft or cross grain at 90° to the selvedge. The diagram below gives a quick and easy reference for rotary cutting the strips required to strip piece the blocks.

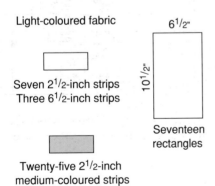

Light-coloured fabric

6½"

Seven 2½-inch strips
Three 6½-inch strips

10½"

Seventeen rectangles

Twenty-five 2½-inch medium-coloured strips

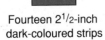

Fourteen 2½-inch dark-coloured strips

Traditionally these quilts were often made from recycled cotton fabrics that were full of family memories and associations. Old dresses and shirts would be carefully unpicked. Any thinning, worn areas would be discarded and the resultant scraps were then sorted into contrasting light, medium, and dark colour values. Occasionally the reverse side of a fabric would be used to assist in the development of a harmonious blend of colour. The patches were then individually cut out from the sorted scraps and pieced together with a light-coloured background fabric that would be used to unify the colour scheme. The diagram below is a cutting guide for the traditional approach using the full-size templates given to mark and cut each patch.

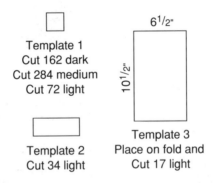

Template 1
Cut 162 dark
Cut 284 medium
Cut 72 light

6½"

10½"

Template 2
Cut 34 light

Template 3
Place on fold and
Cut 17 light

From the light fabric
1   Border A1: cut two strips 2½ x 74 inches.
2   Border A3: cut two strips 8½ x 82 inches.
3   Border B1: cut two strips 2½ x 58 inches.
4   Strip piecing: cut seven 2½-inch strips at 90° to selvedge.
5   Strip piecing: cut three 6½ strips at 90° to selvedge.
6   Rectangles for Block B: cut seventeen rectangles 6½ x 10½ inches.

From the medium fabric
Strip piecing: cut twenty-five 2½-inch strips.

From the dark fabric
1   Border A2: cut two strips 2½ x 78 inches.

2   Border B2: cut two strips 2½ x 6 inches.
3   Strip piecing: cut fourteen 2½ inch strips.
4   Binding: cut nine 2½-inch strips.

From the backing fabric
1   Cut one rectangle 42 x 98 inches.
2   Cut two rectangles 19 x 98 inches

CONSTRUCTION
Strip-piecing guide

Four different sets of strips ar required to construct the block Three sets are used to construct Bloc A. Block B is constructed using th remaining strip set attached to eithe side of a light-coloured rectangle. It vitally important when using spee piecing techniques that a consisten ¼-inch seam allowance is used to c and sew the strips. See the Skill Basi section (page 68) for advice on how mark and sew an accurate ¼-inch sea allowance using the sewing machin Remember to reduce the stitch leng slightly on the sewing machine whe using strip-piecing techniques. A each seam is completed, press th stitching line with a hot dry iron help lock the stitches and smooth th seam line. Then press the sea allowances open.

Strip Set A
1   Sew two dark, two medium an one light strip together as illu trated to make Strip Set A. Pre each seam as it is sewn.
2   Verify that the completed s measures 10½ inches across t short edge. Make three sets.

2½"

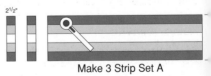

Make 3 Strip Set A

3   Using a rotary cutter slice off 36 x 10½ inch segments.

Strip Set B

Sew three medium and two dark strips together as illustrated below to make Strip Set B. Press each seam as it is sewn.

Make 3 Strip Set B

Verify that the completed set measures 10½ inches across the short edge. Make three sets.
Using a rotary cutter slice off 36 2½ x 10½ inch segments.

Strip Set C

Sew two light, two medium and one dark strip together as illustrated below to make Strip Set C. Press each seam as it is sewn.

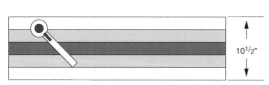

Make 2 Strip Set C

Verify that the completed set measures 10½ inches across the short edge. Make two sets.
Using a rotary cutter slice off 18 2½ x 10½ inch segments.

Block A

Lay out the segments as illustrated and join together to make Block A. Press each seam as it is completed.

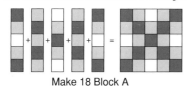

Make 18 Block A

Verify that the completed block measures 10½ x 10½ inches. Make 18 blocks.

Strip Set D

Sew a medium-coloured strip to either side of a 6½-inch wide light-coloured strip to make Strip Set D. Press each seam as it is sewn.
Verify that the completed set measures 10½ inches across the short edge. Make three sets.
Using a rotary cutter slice off 34 2½ x 10½ inch segments.

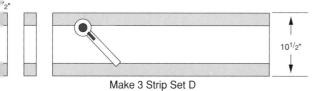

Make 3 Strip Set D

Block B

1 Sew a segment from strip set D to either side of a light-coloured rectangle as illustrated. Press each seam as it is sewn.

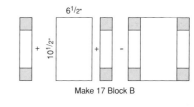

Make 17 Block B

2 Verify that the completed block measures 10½ x 10½ inches.
3 Make 17 blocks.

Completing the top

Row A

Lay out the blocks as illustrated and join to make Row A. Press each seam as it is sewn. Make four Row A.

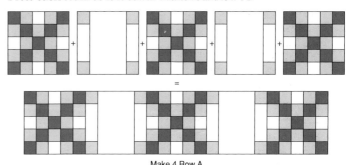

Make 4 Row A

Row B

Lay out the blocks as illustrated and join to make Row B. Press each seam as it is sewn. Make three Row B.

Joining the rows

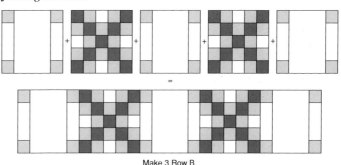

Make 3 Row B

Refer to the main illustration on page 49 and lay out the rows in the sequence illustrated. Join them together row by row and press.

Attaching the borders

It is advisable to measure the quilt top to establish the correct measurements required for the border strips. To avoid wavy edges the dimensions should always be taken through the centre portion of the quilt. Rather than fitting the border to the edge of the quilt, the edge of the quilt is fitted to the border. Refer to the Skill Basics (page 70) for detailed guidance on how to measure and fit borders.

1 Attach an A1 border strip to either side of the quilt as illustrated. Press.
2 Attach a B1 border strip to the top and bottom of the quilt. Press.
3 Attach an A2 border strip to either side of the quilt. Press.
4 Attach a B2 strip to the top and bottom of the quilt. Press.
5 Attach an A3 border strip to either side of the quilt. Press.
6 Attach a B3 strip to the top and bottom of the quilt. Press.

Tidy up the back of the quilt and remove any stray threads that may show through the quilt surface.

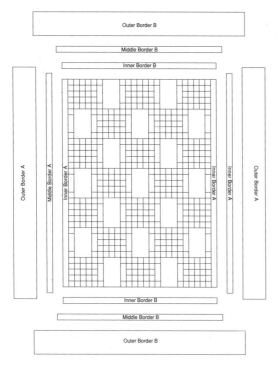

Piecing the backing

The backing consists of three rectangles. Join the rectangles together as illustrated on the next page using a half-inch seam allowance. Snip any selvedge to release the tension along the seam lines. Press.

QUILTING AND FINISHING

The quilt should layered and basted in preparation for quilting. Refer to the Skill Basics section, page 72, if you need help. The quilting designs can be marked on to the surface of the quilt before basting the sandwich. The knot-work

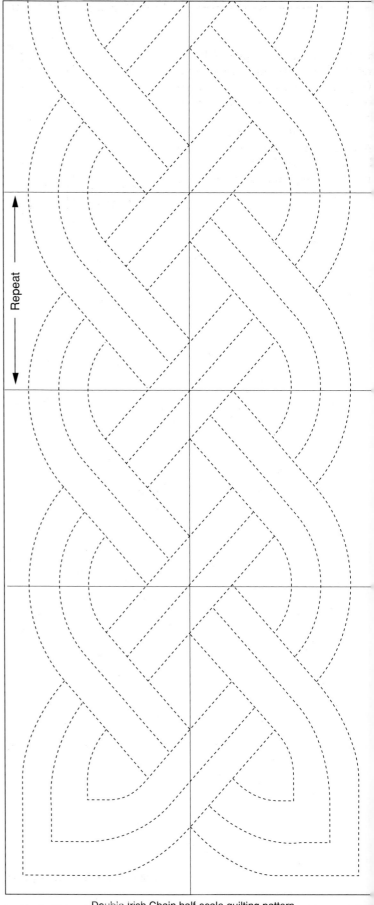

Double Irish Chain half-scale quilting pattern

...otif for the blocks is given full size ...nd the border design will require a ...00 percent enlargement on a photo-...opier to bring it up to the required ...ze.

See the Skill Basics section, page ...4, for advice on attaching a hanging ...eeve and attaching continuous ...rench binding around the edges of ...e quilt.

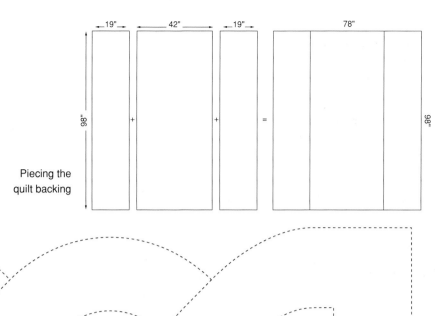

Piecing the quilt backing

Full-scale interlaced quilting motif for Irish Chain

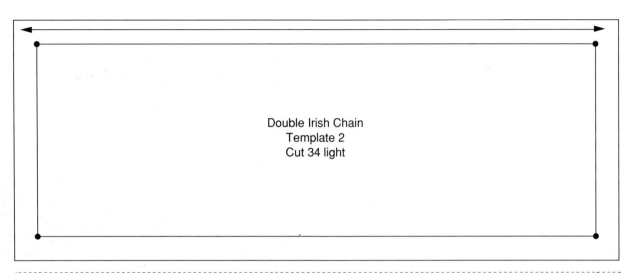

Double Irish Chain
Template 2
Cut 34 light

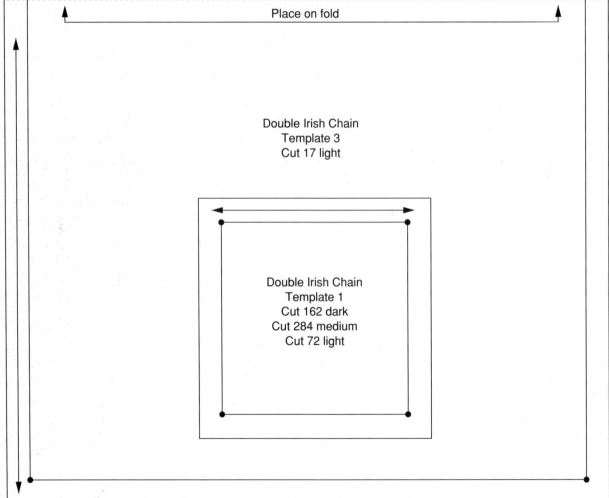

Place on fold

Double Irish Chain
Template 3
Cut 17 light

Double Irish Chain
Template 1
Cut 162 dark
Cut 284 medium
Cut 72 light

CATHEDRAL WINDOW

Squares of background fabrics are folded and stitched to make square 'envelope' shapes. These are then folded again and stab stitched to create smaller squares which are sewn together to create the basic 'frame' block. The 'frames' are formed by folding back and stitching the bias edges of the squares over brightly coloured 'window' patches. The result is a richly textured surface of interlocking curves which requires no wadding, binding or quilting. In the method described, the background fabric is first machined to form the 'envelope' shapes. From this point on the quilt is sewn by hand and can be assembled in small sections at a time.

QUILT SIZE 80 x 100 inches

BLOCK SIZE 4 inches

BLOCKS REQUIRED 500 back ground 'frame' blocks with 955 'window' patches

The quilt illustrated uses just one fabric for the 'frame' blocks and one fabric for the 'window' patches.

However a good mix of scrap silks, cottons and shiny fabrics for the 'window' patches will liven up the surface and make it glow with light. Divide the scraps into contrasting piles of light, medium and dark colour values. Make use of the quarter section design sheet and light, medium and dark-coloured pencils to experiment with the placement of the fabrics. Consider also the use of lightweight patterned fabrics for the 'frame' blocks. The block layout diagram can be used to plan a multicoloured design for the background. For clarity read through all instructions before starting the project.

MATERIALS

(based on 42-inch fabric width)
Background 'frame' fabric: 24 yards
'Window' fabric: 4½ yards

CUTTING

Make sure that the background 'frame' blocks are cut exactly the same size and on the straight grain of the fabric. Half-scale templates are provided.

From the background fabric
Using the Frame template cut 500 squares 8½ x 8½ inches.

From the 'window' fabric
Using the Window template cut 955 squares 2½ x 2½ inches.

CONSTRUCTION

1 Fold an 8½-inch square in half, with right sides together. Sew a ¼-inch seam along each short edge, making a bag shape.

2 Pull the bag open. Align the raw edges and match the seams, placing one on top of the other. Finger-press the seam allowances

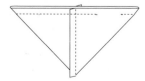

so that they face opposing directions. Pin if required and sew a ¼-inch seam along the long edge, leaving a gap as illustrated.

3 Turn the square right side out through the gap left in the seam. The resulting square looks rather like an envelope. Push out the corners so that they make crisp, sharp angles and press with a hot dry iron, taking care not to stretch the edge of the square, where the fabric is on the bias.

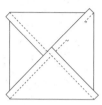 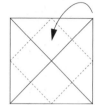

4 Bring one corner of the square down to the centre, as illustrated, and fold the opposite corner to the centre. Starting from the back of the block, take two or three stab stitches with strong thread right through all layers of fabric to secure the points.

5 Bring the remaining corners to the centre and stab stitch again to hold the points firmly Finish the stab stitching securely at the back of the block. Bias edges and the number of folds used can easily cause the corners of the blocks to buckle and distort, especially if the squares have not been cut exactly on the straight grain of the fabric. To overcome the problem, sew a temporary bar-tack across the diagonal of each corner to complete the block. Press each with a hot dry iron. **Note:** the bar-tacks are removed after the blocks have been joined together. Make 500 blocks.

6 Join the blocks by oversewing the edges securely.

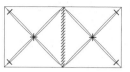

7 Use a tiny dab of water-soluble glue to secure a 'window' patch to the

background. Alternatively, use a pin to hold the fabric. The 'window' patch is centred over the seam joining two adjacent blocks thus hiding the seam from view.

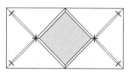

8 Fold back the bias edges to enclose and frame the 'window' patch. Secure the patch to the surface by sewing through the folded frame using either a running stitch or hem stitch.

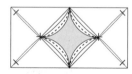

9 The illustration below indicates what a section of joined blocks looks like. The completed quilt requires blocks set 20 x 25, as in the block layout diagram on the next page.

Note: If you enjoy working with lots of different fabrics, use the layout diagram as a design tool to help plan the placement of the window blocks.

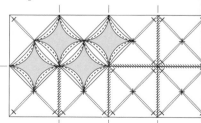

Block layout diagram

Quarter section design sheet

Half-scale
Cathedral Window
Window template
Cut 955 squares

Half-scale
Cathedral Window
Frame template
Cut 500 squares

NINE PATCH STRIPPY

The Nine Patch block is often used to introduce children to patchwork. It is very easy to make. Each block consists of just nine squares arranged in a 3 x 3 grid. Here, seven completed blocks are set on point and pieced together with twelve setting triangles and four corner triangles to create a column. Four of these pieced columns are alternated with five solid strips of fabric (which also create the side borders). Two more strips are attached to the top and bottom of the quilt to complete the top, which is finished with continuous French binding. A speedy strip-piecing method is described for making the blocks. The simplicity of the design lends itself to lots of quilting to give depth and texture to the surface. Template patterns together with full-size quilting motifs are provided. For clarity read through all the instructions before starting the project.

Nine Patch Strippy

QUILT SIZE 78 x 100 inches
BLOCK SIZE 9 inches
BLOCKS REQUIRED 28

MATERIALS
(based on 42-inch fabric width)
Light fabric: 3¼ yards
Medium fabric: 3¼ yards

Dark fabric: 1 yard
Backing fabric: 6¼ yards
Binding fabric: ¼ yard
Wadding: 102 x 108 inches (king size)

CUTTING

Cut the 6-inch wide, medium-coloured strips first. Then use either Method 1 or Method 2 for cutting the fabrics for the blocks. Finally cut the setting and corner triangles, making sure that the grain line is lying in the right direction.

Wide strips and borders
From the medium fabric

1 Cut the strips on the long grain parallel to the selvedge edge.
2 Cut five strips 6 x 89½ inches for the columns and side borders.
3 Cut two strips 6 x 79 inches for the top and bottom borders.

Blocks

Use EITHER Method 1 (for traditional piecing of the pieced columns) OR Method 2 (for rotary cutting and strip piecing the blocks).

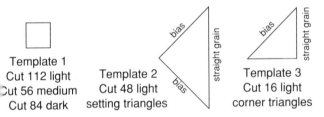

Template 1
Cut 112 light
Cut 56 medium
Cut 84 dark

Template 2
Cut 48 light
setting triangles

Template 3
Cut 16 light
corner triangles

Method 1. Using Template 1 mark and cut:
From the light fabric: 112 squares.
From the medium fabric: 56 squares.
From the dark fabric: 84 squares.

Method 2. Cut the following strips on the weft or cross grain from selvedge to selvedge:
Light fabric: 11 strips 3½ inches wide.
Medium fabric: 5 strips 3½ inches wide.
Dark fabric: 8 strips 3½ inches wide.

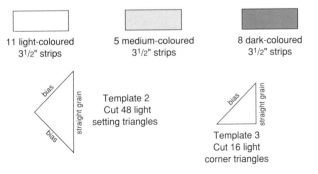

11 light-coloured
3½" strips

5 medium-coloured
3½" strips

8 dark-coloured
3½" strips

Template 2
Cut 48 light
setting triangles

Template 3
Cut 16 light
corner triangles

Setting and corner triangles

Use Templates 2 and 3. Refer to the diagram and double check that the grain line is correct before you cut the triangles, i.e. that the straight grain runs parallel with the long side of Template 2 and that the straight grain runs parallel with the short side of Template 3.

From the light fabric

1 Using Template 2 mark and cut 48 setting triangles.
2 Using Template 3 mark and cut 16 corner triangles.

Quilt backing

From the backing fabric
1 Cut two rectangles 21 x 104 inches.
2 Cut one rectangle 42 x 104 inches.

CONSTRUCTION

Strip piecing the Nine Patch blocks

Two sets of strips are required to construct the blocks. It is vitally important when using speed-piecing techniques that a consistent ¼-inch seam allowance is used to cut and sew the strips. See the Skill Basics section, page 68, for advice on how to mark and sew an accurate ¼-inch seam using the sewing machine. Remember to reduce the stitch length slightly. As each seam is completed, press with a hot, dry iron to help lock the stitches and smooth the seam line. Then press the seam allowance open.

Strip Set A

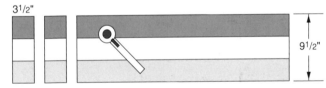

Make 5 Strip Set A

1 Sew one dark and one medium strip to either side of a light-coloured strip, as illustrated. Press each seam as it is sewn.
2 Verify that the completed set measures 9½ inches across the short edge.
3 Make five of Strip Set A.
4 Using a rotary cutter slice off 56 3½ x 9½ inch segments.

Strip Set B

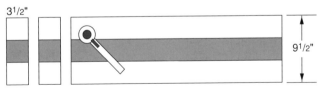

Make 3 Strip Set B

1 Sew a light strip to either side of a dark strip to make Strip Set B. Press each seam as it is sewn.
2 Verify that the completed set measures 9½ inches across the short edge.

3 Make three of Strip Set B.

4 Using a rotary cutter slice off 28 3½ x 9½ inch segments.

Completing the blocks

1 Set out the segments as illustrated and sew together row by row to complete the block.

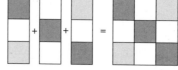

Make 28 design blocks

2 Verify that the completed block measures 9½ x 9½ inches.

3 Make 28 blocks.

Piecing the columns

1 Refer to the illustration here and join one setting triangle and two corner triangles to a block as illustrated to make Unit A. Press

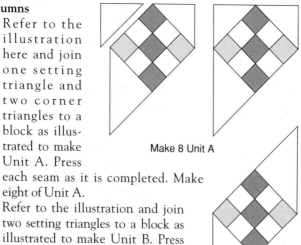

Make 8 Unit A

each seam as it is completed. Make eight of Unit A.

2 Refer to the illustration and join two setting triangles to a block as illustrated to make Unit B. Press each seam as it is completed. Make twenty of Unit B.

3 Arrange five Unit As and two Unit Bs, as illustrated, to construct a column. Make four columns. (See illustration, right.)

Completing the top (see top illustration, facing page)

1 Join a long strip to either side of one column.

2 Join a long strip to one side of the three remaining columns, as illustrated.

3 Join the sections and add the top and bottom border strips.

4 Press and tidy any stray threads.

QUILTING AND FINISHING
Marking the quilt top

It is important, before marking the fabric for quilting, to test the chosen marker to be sure it serves the purpose required. Though it is often still possible to see where antique quilts were marked, it is not considered acceptable for any markings to be visible on the surface of contemporary quilts. Different markers respond differently on different fabrics. See the Skill Basics section, page 67, for further details.

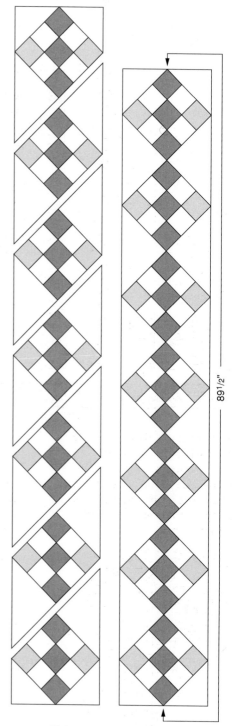

89½"

Make 4 Nine Patch columns

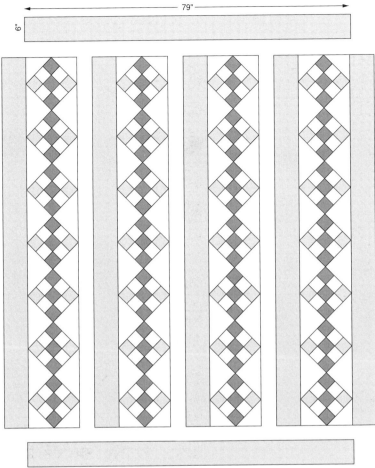

79"

6'

Completing the top

A window light box

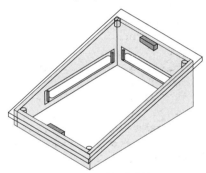

An easy to make light box

1 The straight linear design is easily marked either by using masking tape or by using a rotary ruler to guide the line marker. Mark the lines parallel to the seam line and ½ inch apart from each other. (See illustration below.)

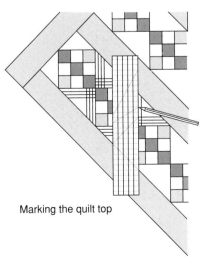

Marking the quilt top

2 Make templates to aid the marking process of the curved leaf patterns.

3 Make a paper pattern of the spiral heart motif. Use a black felt tip pen to create a heavy outline onto the paper.

4 Check that the ink has dried before using the pattern! Place it under the fabric to be marked so that the pattern outline is visible, and trace the design onto the fabric using the selected and tested fabric marker. Some fabrics will require a light source to reveal the pattern outline. In many cases a window pane will provide suffi-cient light. This simple method is useful enough for tracing single motifs, but is rather awkward if there is a lot of marking to do. A glass-topped coffee tables illumi-nated with a lamp from below will make a more comfortable substi-

tute. (Very efficient light boxes are easily constructed from block board using small, low-wattage, fluorescent light strips and a sheet of frosted perspex.)

Take great care when marking the quilt top and remember not to use the iron once the top is marked. Heat will cause the mark-ings to become permanent. For this reason keep the work away from direct sunlight and heated radiators.

Piecing the backing (see overleaf)
The backing consists of three rectan-gles. Join the rectangles together as illustrated, using ½-inch seam allowances. Snip any selvedges to release the tension along the seam lines.

QUILTING AND FINISHING

The quilt is layered and basted in preparation for the quilting process. Refer to the Skill Basics section, page 72, if you need help.

See the Skills Basics section, page 74, for advice on making a hanging sleeve and attaching a continuous French binding around the edges of the quilt.

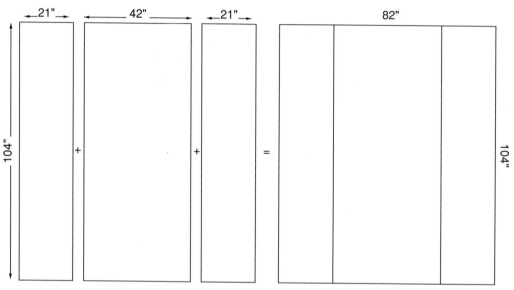

Piecing the quilt backing

Nine Patch Strippy
Cut 112 light
Cut 56 medium
Cut 84 dark

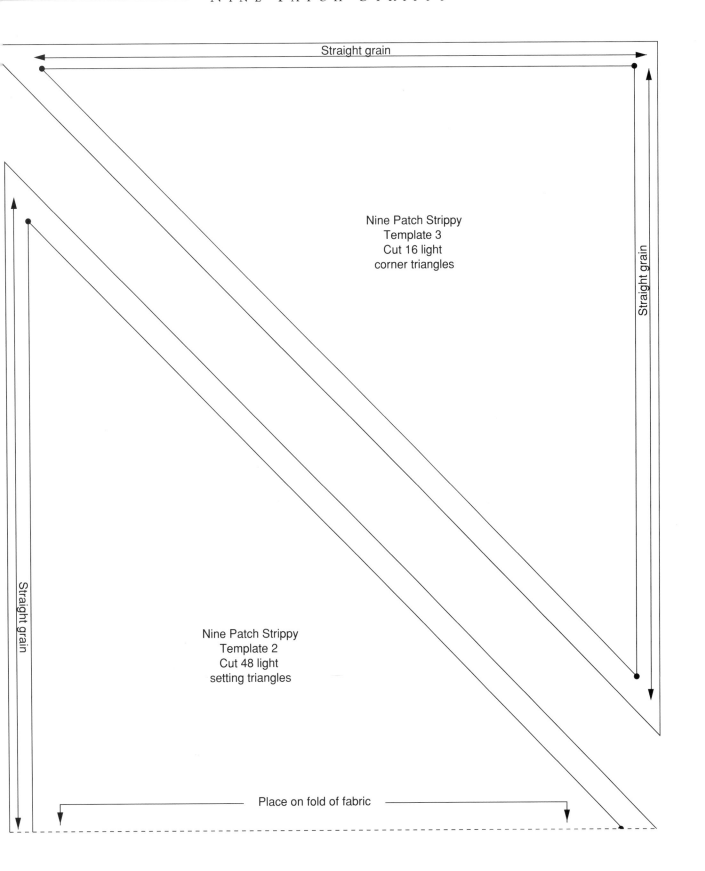

Straight grain

Straight grain

Nine Patch Strippy
Template 3
Cut 16 light
corner triangles

Straight grain

Nine Patch Strippy
Template 2
Cut 48 light
setting triangles

Place on fold of fabric

Quilting motif

Skill Basics

Contents

This section provides full details of techniques used in the projects in this book. Experienced patchworkers will find it useful when working on their own designs.

SEWING KIT

A basic sewing kit for patchwork includes:

Needles Betweens are the traditional quilting needles. Number 8 is a good size to start with. The higher the number, the smaller and finer the needle. Straws are used for basting and Sharps for general piecing and appliqué work.

Thimbles Use one that fits well and has a raised edge around the rim.

Pins Sharp, shiny slender dressmakers' pins. Specialist, slender flower-headed pins are a luxury well worth having. Put them on your family wish-list if you feel they are an extravagance.

Scissors Sharp fabric scissors, embroidery scissors, thread snips.

Toning thread Ecru is a good staple colour as are shades of grey and brown.

A good-sized seam ripper – not just for unpicking seams but also helpful for guiding the patches through the sewing machine.

CUTTING EQUIPMENT

The rotary cutter has revolutionised the whole patchwork process and comes in two sizes. The larger one is best for patchwork. They have extremely sharp circular blades and should be handled with care. Some have straight handles, others have curved handles, and some are equipped with spring-loaded safety guards. Keep all cutters in a safe place, well away from tiny fingers.

Whatever type you buy, always roll the cutter away from you and be sure to replace the safety guard every time a cut is finished.

Rotary ruler These rulers are made of thick transparent plastic and are used to guide the rotary cutter. They come in a bewildering variety of types. The best to buy are the 6 x 24-inch Omnigrid rulers. They have both yellow and black markings making a horizontal and vertical grid at ⅛-inch intervals. They are also marked with 30°, 45° and 60°. The grid and the angles enable the ruler to be used both as a T-square and as a right angle.

Some patchworkers have a collection of rotary rulers – the Trudy Hughes Rotary Mate is a very useful size for cutting smaller pieces.

Cutting mat The mat is essential to protect both the table top and the blade of the rotary cutter. A useful size is 24 x 18 inches. Make sure that the mat you buy has a grid marked on it which is helpful when straightening the fabric. Some mats are marked with 45° lines, which are useful when cutting bias strips.

Fabric-cutting scissors If you are not yet ready to make the investment in rotary cutting equipment make sure that your fabric shears are well sharpened. Never allow fabric-cutting scissors to be used for cutting paper or template-making material.

Embroidery scissors A small pair of scissors is useful for trimming seams and for appliqué work. Test the scissors to make sure that the blades will cut right up to the tips.

Paper-cutting scissors Keep a pair of scissors for cutting paper, card and template plastic.

SEWING MACHINE

Buy the best you can afford. Just remember it is not necessary to buy a

top-of-the-range computerised mode The minimum features to look for are
- **First-class easily adjustab tension**
- **Easily adjustable stitch length**
- **A good even straight stitch**
- **A good satin stitch**
- **An invisible hem stitch.**

Highly desirable features include:
- **A feed dog that will disengage allow free-motion sewing**
- **A variable needle stop positio (either up or down)**
- **A two-speed motor**
- **A walking foot**
- **A ¼-inch foot.**

Avoid machines where the tensio and the stitch length are not eas adjustable. Take along the kind fabric you will use to have a test r on a possible purchase. If the dealer not happy for you to try the machi then do not buy it.

Read your manual, clean ar de-fluff the machine regularly, chan needles frequently, have it serviced a reputable dealer.

FABRIC SELECTION

Choose 100 percent cottons for ease use. Avoid polycottons, they are stu born, unforgiving and difficult to se Silks look stunning in patchwork. T most suitable is Honan silk which quite stable and does not fray as eas as other varieties. If recycling mate als, choose the best parts and ruthles discard worn, frayed or thinning bits.

FABRIC PREPARATION

Whether you decide to pre-wa fabric is a personal decision. It is w to test for colour fastness especially dark red and blue colours, which a notoriously fugitive dyes. To stabil soft, floppy fabrics, use spray starch

...ve a good crisp finish which will ...eatly aid precision in marking and ...ecing. If the starch is not sufficient, ...y using the lightest-weight iron-on ...terfacing to give some body.

...ABRIC MARKING

...ifferent types of fabric will require ...fferent types of marker, depending ...n the colour and pattern. The most ...seful are: HB pencils, silver pencils, ...alk markers, water-soluble blue ...ns, waterproof ink pens, and when ...l else fails a fineline ballpoint. ...lways test your chosen marker to be ...ertain it will meet your requirements.

Lay the template **face down** on the **...rong** side of the fabric making sure ...at the straight grain aligns with the ...ainline marking on the template. ...race around the template shape as ...ccurately as possible, and make dot ...arks at the seam junctions where ...ppropriate.

...AKING TEMPLATES

...emplates are best made from easily-...t vinyl or plastic sheets. They can ...e made from manilla card or card-...oard, but these are not so durable.

Secure a piece of tracing paper over the pattern with some low-tack masking tape. Carefully trace the pattern shape. These traced lines are the seam lines. Mark a dot at each corner.

Use a ruler to draft the ¼-inch allowance all the way round the shape. This second line is the cutting line. Carefully peel away the masking tape and remove the tracing paper.

Glue the tracing paper to the template material (if plastic, check the glue is suitable).

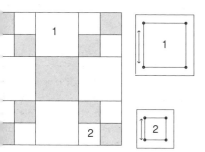

4 *Carefully cut out the template on the* **outer** *(cutting) line. Using an awl (and a piece of waste wood to protect the table top) pierce a hole through the dots marked at each seam junction. Smooth the back of the holes with fine sandpaper and test that it is possible to mark a dot onto fabric, through the hole in the template (see illustration).*

5 *Label each template with its number, block name, and direction of grain.*

ROTARY CUTTING

Generally, when using the rotary cutter, the fabric is cut in strips from selvedge edge to selvedge edge (on the cross or weft grain). First it is important to straighten the edge of the fabric so the strips will be cut straight and at right angles to the selvedge edges. Guidelines are given for a right-handed method.

Straightening the edge of the fabric

1 *Fold the fabric selvedge to selvedge and press the fold. Fold in half again by aligning the fold against the selvedge edges, making four layers of fabric. Press the new fold.*

2 *Line up the folded edge of the fabric with a line on the cutting board with the bulk of the fabric to your left (see illustration).*

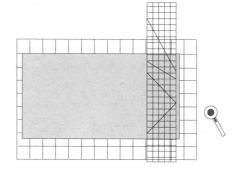

3 *Place the ruler at right angles to the selvedge and align it with the markings on the edges of the cutting mat.*

4 *Place your left hand on the ruler, press down firmly holding the cutter in your right hand. Slide the cutter along the bottom of the board from right to left until it hits the ruler.*

5 *Release the safety catch and take a*

smooth firm cut away from yourself, keeping the blade of the cutter tight against the edge of the ruler. Return the safety guard as soon as the cut is made.

6 *Turn the mat around so that the bulk of the fabric is now on your right-hand side and you are ready to start cutting strips the width you require (see illustration).*

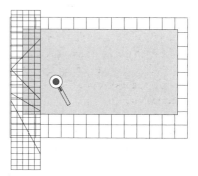

HAND SEWING
Piecing the blocks
Analyse the block to see how it can best be sewn. Sew the smallest patches into small units first. Then join the units into rows, and finally join the rows to complete the block.

Hand piecing
After the fabric pieces have been cut and marked lay them out in the sequence they will be pieced. Use neutral-coloured threads. Beige or ecru and mid greys are good staple colours. When sewing a dark patch to a light one match the thread to the fabric towards which you will be pressing the seam allowance. Generally sew the tiny pieces into small units first. Then sew the units into rows, and finally join the rows to complete the block.

The simple seam
The hand-pieced simple seam is a

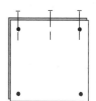

straight seam joining two patches together. It runs from dot to dot along the seam line. To join two patches place them right sides together. Pin them together exactly on the marked dots, placing the pins at right angles to the sewing line. Start the seam line at the dot and take one or two back stitches to secure. Sew with a small running stitch right through the dot, and take another backstitch every two or three stitches. Remove any pins as you go, finishing the seam with a couple of back stitches at the dot marking the end of the seam. Press towards the darker fabric.

The seam joint

A seam joint occurs where two or more seams cross or converge. For example in the four patch, four seams meet at the centre of the block. Align and pin two units of joined squares together and pin at the dots. Place a further pin the

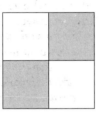

centre of the seam, exactly at the point where the opposing seams butt up against each other. Begin the seam at the dot mark with a couple of short backstitches and sew with short running stitches to the pin at the butted seam. Hold the seam allowance out of the way and take a small back-

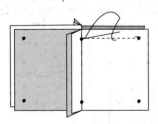

stitch. Do not sew across the seam allowance, just slip the needle through

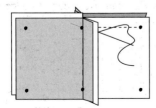

the seam. Flip the seam allowances towards the seam just sewn and continue sewing. End the seam at the dot mark with a couple of back-stitches. Machine-sewn seams are sewn from edge to edge.

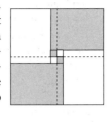

MACHINE PIECING

Accurate cutting is required for machine piecing, which is why templates for machine piecing always include the seam allowances. The rotary cutter is a great aid in precision, and it is essential that the ¼-inch seam allowance on your sewing machine exactly matches the ¼-inch seam allowance used when cutting the fabric.

Quarter-inch seam allowance

If the presser foot on your machine is ¼ inch wide, align the cut edge of the fabric with the edge of the presser foot. Seams are generally sewn from edge to edge of the fabric. Set in seams are an exception to this rule.

If a ¼-inch presser foot is not available it is help-ful to mark the ¼-inch allow-ance on your machine with a piece of masking tape to guide the edge of the fabric (see illustration).

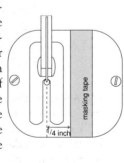

Chain piecing simple seams

Organise the patches in the sequence they are to be pieced and wherever possible chain piece to save time and thread. Place the patches right sides together and sew a seam from edge to edge. Do not remove

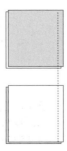

the patches from the sewing machine. Place the next pair of patches under the presser foot and sew as seam from edge to edge. Continue this sequence until all the patches are sewn. As the process is continued a long line of patches like a miniature line of bunting is produced. Use thread snip-pers to snip the thread between each unit.

TYPES OF SEAM
Joints and points; pin stabbing

Joints and points occur where two or more seam lines converge. The extra bulk of the fabric meeting the feed dogs of the machine makes pin stab-bing a must for precision seam match-ing. The illustration below shows pin

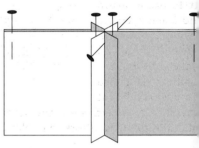

stabbing at the seam joint on a four patch unit. Stab the pin right through the seam line of the matching patches and pull it through tightly. Hold the patches together firmly, peel back the seam allowances to confirm that the seam lines are still perfectly aligned and secure a further two pins, one on each side of the stabbed pin and as close as possible to it. Remove the stab pin and sew a perfectly matching seam.

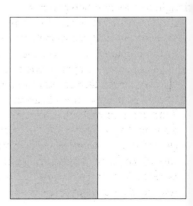

Where a pointed angled seam hits seam line as in this illustration, aim

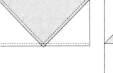

the needle of the machine to pass directly through the middle of the X junction formed by the stitching lines.

Set in seams

A set in seam occurs where two patches form an angle into which a third patch is inserted.

They are sometimes referred to as 'Y' seams. With a little preparation and some accurate sewing they are not difficult to piece. Make sure that the patches to be pieced are accurately cut and have dots marked on the seam junction points as illustrated below.

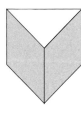

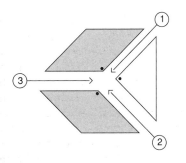

The example given shows the sequence of sewing when setting in a triangle to two diamond patches.

Refer to the illustration (next column) and with the triangle on top of the diamond patch sew the first seam from the edge of the fabric to the dot mark. Backstitch at this point and do not sew into the seam allowance.

Turn the unit and place the second diamond patch underneath the triangle and sew the second seam from the edge of the fabric up to the dot mark. Backstitch at this point and do not sew into the seam allowance.

3 *Align the edges of the diamonds and sew the final seam from the edge of the fabric up to the dot mark and backstitch to finish the set in seam.*

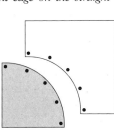

Curved seams

Machine piecing curves is not so difficult but does require accurate templates with balance marks along the curves. The example gives the stages in marking, cutting and sewing a Drunkard's Path patch.

1 *Place the two templates required, face down on the wrong side of the fabric with the straight edge on the straight grain. Cut out the fabric shapes accurately along the marked lines and clearly mark the balance points.*

2 *With right sides together place the small convex patch on top of the concave piece. Pin through the centre balance marks, weaving the pin in and out twice to secure it.*

3 *Pin either end of the curve through the balance marks, aligning the straight edges before pinning.*

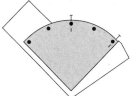

Pin each end of the curve

4 *Pin twice more, carefully matching the balance marks, easing the piece as you secure the patches.*

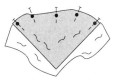

5 *Sew with a ¼-inch seam allowance, Press the seam allowance towards the concave curve.*

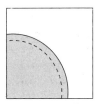

Half way seams

Half way seams are partially sewn seams that avoid the necessity of setting in a seam. They occur in blocks like the one illustrated.

1 *Begin with the centre square A. Align strip B with the bottom of the square and sew a seam half way along the side of the*

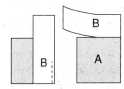

square and back tack. Rotate the unit 90° to the left (anticlockwise).

2 *Place strip C on top of the square and sew the seam from edge to edge. Rotate the unit 90° to the left.*

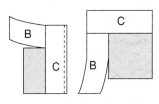

3 *Place strip D on top of the square and sew the seam from edge to edge as*

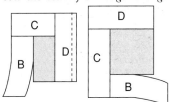

illustrated. Turn the unit 90° to the left.

4   *Repeat the process with strip E.*

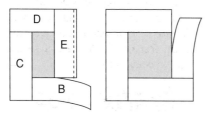

5   *Complete the seam along the edge of strip B to complete the partial seam unit.*

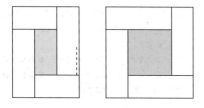

PRESSING

The aim is to have the fabric surface as smooth as possible. The nature of the fabric and type of construction method used will dictate what strategy to use for pressing seams. In general terms it is advisable to press the seam allowances to one side where hand piecing has been used. If you use the sewing machine you will probably discover that a combination of pressing seams open and pressing to one side will work for you .

SETTING THE BLOCKS TOGETHER

There are many ways of setting the blocks together – here are two of the most popular.

Straight sets
Blocks are set side by side in rows.

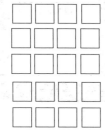

1   *Lay the blocks out on a flat surface to check positioning.*

2   *Sew together each row of blocks as illustrated, pin stabbing and basting to match joints and points perfectly.*

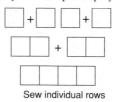

Sew individual rows

4   *Sew the rows together into sections.*

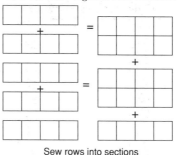

Sew rows into sections

5   *Join the sections to complete the top.*

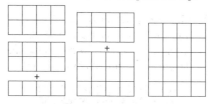

Diagonal sets
Blocks are turned on point and set together diagonally. Setting and corner triangles are used around the edges to complete the rectangular shape.

1   *Lay the blocks out on a flat surface to check positioning.*

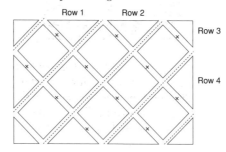
Row 1   Row 2   Row 3   Row 4

2   *Sew one row at a time as illustrated. It is wise to replace the blocks to their places in the row each time a seam is sewn.*

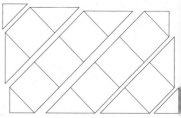

3   *Lay out all the sewn rows in sequenc￵ and sew each row together. Check th￵ position of the sequence after eac￵ seam has been sewn and finally attac￵ the remaining corner triangles t￵ complete the piecing of the top.*

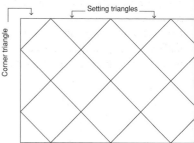
Corner triangle   Setting triangles

BORDERS

Measuring and cutting borders
To enable the quilt to hang square th￵ borders should be cut the same lengt￵ as measurements taken through th￵ centre of the top. Because of th￵ tendency of the edges of a pieced to￵ to stretch it is important not to us￵ the edge measurements. Directions ar￵ given for fitting the three most popu￵ lar types of border.

Straight borders
1   *Borders are cut to the finished widt￵ plus seam allowances. To determin￵ the length to be cut, measure length ￵ through the centre. To this measure￵ ment add 2 inches for a workin￵ allowance and cut two borders th￵ length.*

Measure length A through the centre. Add 2" working allowance

Mark the centre of the long edges by folding the quilt in half (so the top and bottom edges meet), then pin-mark

the centre point of the edge. Fold a border strip in half and mark its centre with a securely fastened pin. Measure in each direction from the centre of the border strip half the measurement determined in step 1. Weave a pin in and out to mark each spot. Repeat the process with the second long border strip.

Lay one of the border strips on top of the long edge of the quilt matching the pins to the centre and the corner edge

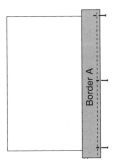

of the quilt top. Pin baste along the edges – it may be necessary to ease the quilt top to fit the borders.

Use a rotary ruler or right angle to square the borders with the quilt top as illustrated and trim the excess fabric with a rotary cutter.

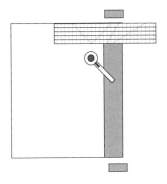

Measure length B across the centre (including the attached border strips) and add 2 inches as a working allowance.

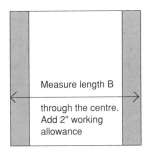

Measure length B through the centre. Add 2" working allowance

6 Cut two borders this length and repeat steps 2–4 to complete the border.

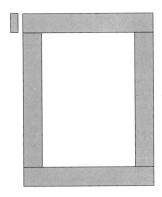

Borders with corner squares

1 Borders are cut the finished width plus seam allowances. To determine the length to be cut, measure length A

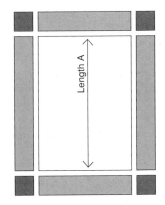

Length A

through the centre. To this measurement add 2 inches for a working allowance and cut two borders this length. The width will be the finished width of the border plus ½ inch for the seam allowances.

2 Mark the centre of the long edges by folding the quilt in half (so the top and bottom edges meet), then pin-mark the centre point of the edge. Fold a

border strip in half and mark its centre with a securely fastened pin. Measure in each direction from the centre of the border strip half the measurement determined in step 1. Weave a pin in and out to mark the spot. Repeat the process with the second border strip.

3 Lay one of the border strips on top of the edge of the quilt matching the pins to the centre and corner edge of the quilt top. Pin-baste along the edges, easing the quilt top where necessary to fit the borders.

4 Use a rotary ruler or right angle to square the borders with the quilt top and trim the excess fabric.

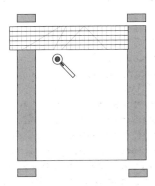

5 Measure length B through the centre of the quilt. Cut two border strips to this dimension plus ½ inch for the seam allowances. Attach corner squares to either end of each strip.

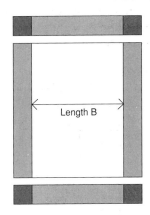

Length B

6 Lay a border strip on top of the quilt top and pin baste, matching the seam allowances and easing the quilt top where necessary. Repeat with the final border strip to complete the quilt top.

Mitred borders

These always look good with diagonal sets and with striped border fabric. They are cut the length of the quilt, plus twice the finished width of the border, plus 4 inches working allowance. The width to cut is the finished width, plus seam allowances.

1 Press the quilt top and make a dot mark ¼ inch in from each of the four corners. See illustration and measure length A through the centre of the quilt. Mark the centre of the long edges by folding the quilt in half

Length A

(so the top and bottom edges meet), then pin-mark the centre of the edge.

2 Fold one of the long border strips in half and pin to mark the centre. Measure in each direction from the centre, and pin mark half the measurement determined in step 1.

3 Mark a dot on the seam line ¼ inch in from the marker pins to indicate the start and finish of the seam line.

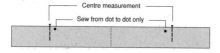

Centre measurement
Sew from dot to dot only

Fold, pin and mark the second border strip in the same way.

4 Measure across the centre of the quilt to establish dimension B.

5 Fold one of the remaining border strips in half and pin to mark the centre. Measure out in each direction from the centre, half the measurement determined in step 4 and pin mark. Mark the seam dots on each strip as in step 3. Fold, pin and mark the remaining border strip in the same way.

6 Starting at the centre pins and with a border strip on top, pin baste the border strip to the quilt top. Match the pins to the centre of the top and pin stab the seam dots to secure the border. Complete the pin basting, easing the quilt top where required to the border strip. Start and stop the seam on the marked dots. Do not sew into the seam allowance at the corner

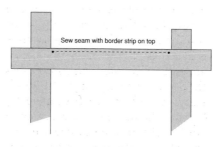

Sew seam with border strip on top

points. Begin and end each seam with a back tack. Repeat this process until all the borders are attached to the top.

Marking the mitre

For this next step you will require a rotary ruler that has a 45° angle marked on it (as illustrated).

1 Press the seams and the entire top. Smooth out the top wrong side up on a flat surface. Starting at one of the bottom corners, adjust the border strips so that the side border strip folds back diagonally on itself, lying parallel to the bottom strip. Pin if necessary to secure, then press.

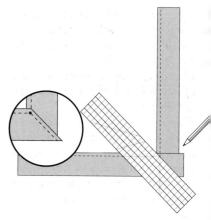

2 Align the 45° marking of the ruler o the quilt top, with the edge of the rul crossing through the seam dot as illu trated. Mark a diagonal line on th border strip to indicate the seam line.

3 Baste the seam from the inner dot the outer edge of the quilt. Chec from the front to ensure the corner hanging straight and make any fir adjustments necessary before pressir the seam and sewing on the crease line to complete the corner.

QUILTING
Basting the sandwich

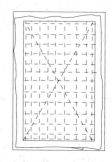

The quilt sandwich consists of th completed top, the wadding and backing fabric. Many kinds of waddin are available: 2-oz polyester wadding i suitable for a beginner. Like the back ing, wadding should be cut 2 inche larger all round than the quilt top The backing fabric should be of simi lar weight to and in harmony with th quilt top. Avoid having a sear running down the centre of the lining

Use a scratchproof table top to la out the sandwich. The quilt is baste to prevent the layers from shiftin during the quilting process. Use white basting thread to avoid coloured fibres becoming trapped in the surface of the quilt and in the wadding.

1 *Use masking tape to mark the centre of the table top and also mark the centre point of each of the sides.*

2 *Thoroughly press the quilt top and tidy any stray thread that may show through (the last thing you want is to have dark wisps of thread trapped and visible in the sandwich when you have finished quilting and binding the quilt).*

3 *The quilting design may be marked either before or after the sandwich is basted. A complicated feather design is likely to be marked prior to basting, unless stencils are used to mark it from the top.*

4 *Fold the backing fabric in two with wrong sides together. Fold in two again. Mark the centre point with a loose tacking thread that is easily removable. Also mark the centre point of each edge with a sharp crease.*

5 *Place the centre point of the backing on to the marked centre of the table and carefully unfold the fabric, making sure that it lies square on the table, aligning the halfway creases with the masking tape. Clamp in place with cloth clamps or with bull-dog clips (the ones with long arms that fold back on themselves).*

6 *Fold the wadding into four and thread mark the centre in the same way as the backing. Put the centre fold on the marked centre of the backing and gently unfold the wadding smoothing it out with a yardstick. Be careful not to stretch the wadding at all. Undo the clamps and reclamp the two layers together.*

7 *Fold the quilt top in two, right sides together and then fold again and light-ly crease the centre of the sides. Match the centre to the centre of the wadding. Gently unfold the quilt top over the wadding, being careful to keep it square. Use a wooden yard rule to gently smooth out any bumps. Unclamp and then reclamp the three layers together.*

8 *From the centre out baste diagonal rows of basting stitches towards each corner of the table. Use a dessert spoon to help with the basting process, by placing it firmly on the quilt sand-wich, just in front of where you wish the needle to emerge. Make the bast-ing stitches around 1 inch long.*

9 *Continue the basting in straight lines horizontally and vertically creating a grid of rows about 3–4 inches apart. As each area is completed, unclamp and slide it across the table top ready for the next area to be basted Starting with the backing fabric smooth the layers over the table top, one by one. Reclamp and continue this process until the basting is complete.*

10 *Finish off with a row of small basting stitches right around the edges of the quilt.*

Hand quilting

The purpose of the quilting stitch is to firmly lock the layers of the quilt together. A simple running stitch is generally used. Sometimes the stitches are extremely small, and sometimes they are extremely large. Although small stitches are favoured by 'experts' the size of the stitch is not so crucial. The important thing is to aim to make the stitches as even and as regular as possible. It helps to wear a thimble on the middle finger of the sewing hand and one on the forefinger of the other hand to stop the needle pricking your finger.

Quilting needles

Betweens are the traditional choice of hand quilters. A number eight is a suitable size for beginners. The higher the number the finer and shorter the needle. A short needle helps to keep the stitches small and evenly spaced.

Quilting thread

Specialised thread is available in a good range of colours. 100% cotton thread is the favourite, although poly-cotton threads are often used. Cut short lengths of around 18 inches to sew with. Knot the cut end of the

thread, and pull the thread through the fabric in the same direction that the needle is travelling to avoid excess friction creating tangled threads.

Quilting designs

There are many sources for quilt designs. Often pieced blocks are outline quilted about ¼ inch around the patches. The illustrations given show outline quilting for some blocks, together with some traditional filler and border designs.

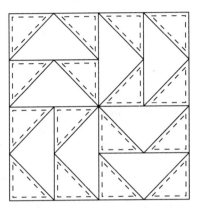

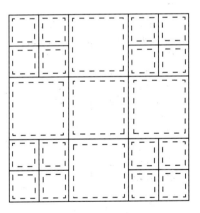

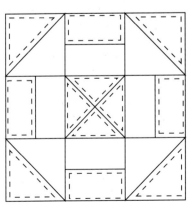

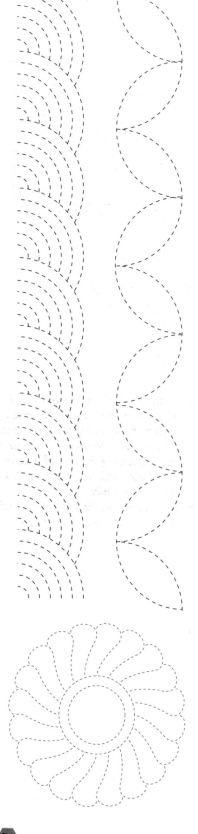

FINISHING

Hanging sleeve

The time to fix a hanging sleeve to a quilt is when the quilting is completed, the excess wadding and backing have been trimmed, and before the binding is applied. The depth of the sleeve will be determined by the depth of the batten you use to display the quilt.

1 *Determine the width of the quilt top, and plan to have the sleeve to finish around two or three inches narrower than this dimension.*

2 *Cut a strip of cloth 6 inches wide by the required length. Fold in half, right sides together along the long edge and, using a ½-inch seam allowance, sew two seams along each short edge.*

3 *Turn right sides out, align the raw edges and press the seams and along the entire length of the sleeve. Fold in half lengthwise and finger press to mark the centre point.*

4 *Match the centre point of the raw edged side of the sleeve to the centre point of the quilt edge and pin baste along the top. Sew a scant ¼-inch seam along the edge to secure. Pin baste the lower edge of the sleeve and slip stitch to the quilt, making sure the stitches do not go through to the front of the quilt.*

Continuous French binding

This is a strong and durable binding. It can be made from both straight cut and bias cut strips. Straight strips should be cut from selvedge to selvedge along the weft grain. The weft has greater elasticity than the warp or long grain and helps to give the binding a smooth, tailored look.

1 *Cut sufficient 2½-inch strips, selvedge to selvedge to go around the perimeter of the quilt, plus an extra 14 inches.*

2 *The strips are joined by cutting the ends of each strip at 45° with a rotary*

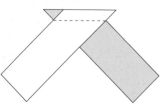

ruler and joining one to the other a right angles along the bias edge. You will notice that as the strips are placed at right angles to each other a triangle appears at either edge. The seam should run exactly between the spots where the triangles emerge from the long edges of the strips.

3 *Mark a line parallel to, and 1 inch away from the bias edge on the wrong side of the fabric.*

4 *Fold the long edges of the binding wrong sides together along the long edge and press with a hot iron to make a sharp crease along the folded edge.*

5 *Align the raw edges of the binding strip on the right side of the quilt edge. Start with the marked end of the binding strips, half way down one of the long sides. Leave a spare 6–7 inch tail of binding before starting to sew the binding to the quilt top. Start with a few back stitches to secure the seam and use a generous ¼-inch seam allowance.*

6 *Stop sewing exactly ¼ inch from the corner of the quilt and sink the needle at this spot. Lift the presser foot. Pivot the quilt 90°. Let down the presser foot and reverse stitch in a straight line off the edge of the quilt.*

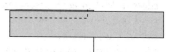

Cut the thread.

7 *Fold the binding strip back on itself, 90° away from the horizontal edge of the quilt making a diagonal fold at the corner. Use a seam ripper or similar tool to hold the fold securely and fold the binding back down towards you so that the raw edges are now parallel with the vertical edge of the quilt. Use the*

seam ripper to ease the fold so that it extends very slightly beyond the edge just sewn.

8 Sink the needle and sew from the horizontal edge until you reach the point ¼ inch away from the next corner where steps 6 and 7 are repeated. Continue the process until all four corners are complete.

9 Carry on sewing around the final corner and stop the seam at approximately 12 inches distance from the original starting point. Take a couple of back stitches to secure. Cut the binding leaving a tail of around 7 inches.

10 Take the binding strip with the pencil mark 1 inch from the edge and smooth it along the edge of the quilt. Lay the second binding tail on top of the marked strip. At the pencil mark fold the top strip back on itself along the marked line, opening out each strip. Finger press and cut the second strip on the fold line. Align the two

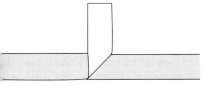

edges at 90° to each other and with small stitches tack a ½-inch seam. Refold the joined strips on the long edge and test to ensure that the binding lies flatly on the quilt surface. Make any adjustments necessary. Machine sew the short joining seam

and then complete the seam sewing the binding to the quilt.

11 Turn the binding to the back of the quilt and slipstitch along the folded edge taking care that the stitches do not penetrate the surface of the quilt top. At each corner fold the fabric to make tiny mitred corners which you

may or may not slipstitch as you please.

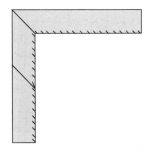

Bias binding

Bias binding is applied to a quilt edge using exactly the same construction methods as above. The only difference is that the 2½-inch wide fabric strips are cut on the bias. Bias binding uses lots of fabric and if used on a straight edge often gives a rippled twisted look. It is best used only for curved edges.

Continuous bias binding

1 Cut a square in half diagonally.

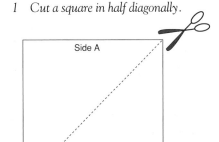

2 Align side A and side B right sides together and sew a ¼-inch seam along the edge.

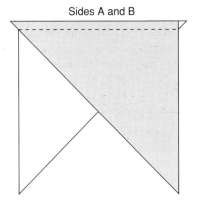

3 Press the seam open. With a long ruler mark 2½-inch strips parallel to the bias edge.

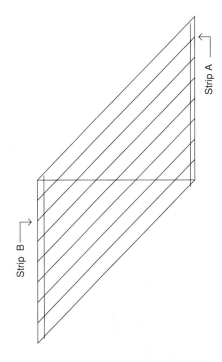

4 Mark a ¼-inch seam line parallel to the straight grain edges as illustrated.

5 Offset the seam by one strip width joining strip A to strip B. Pin baste at each junction of the marked strips and seam line, and sew along the seam line to form a tube.

6 Start cutting the bias strip at one end, rolling the tube around as you go.

SPEED CUTTING AND PIECING TECHNIQUES

Rotary cutting equipment can greatly speed up the cutting of rectangles and some triangles. It must, however, be used accurately, and it is important to use a consistent seam allowance – ¼ inch is the standard, and is used throughout this book (see page 68). Before cutting, therefore, it helps to recognise and calculate both the finished size and the cut size of a shape. The finished size of a shape does not include the size of the seam allowances. The cut size includes the measurement of the standard ¼-inch seam allowance. The following formulae make it easy to determine the cut dimensions of the most commonly occurring shapes in block patchwork.

Squares

The finished size of a square is determined by the measurement of one of its sides.

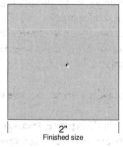

2"
Finished size

The cut size of a square is calculated by adding ½ inch to the finished size.

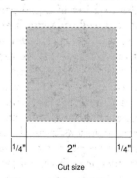

¼"   2"   ¼"

Cut size

Speed cutting squares

For example: to the finished size of a 2-inch square add seam allowances (¼ inch + ¼ inch) or ½ inch for a cut size of 2½ inches.

Speed piecing Four Patch squares

1 *Cut one 2½-inch strip of light fabric from selvedge to selvedge, and one of contrasting fabric.*
2 *Place the fabrics with right sides facing and using a short stitch setting and a ¼-inch seam allowance, join the strips along one long side.*

3 *Press the closed seam to lock the stitches, then open out and press the seam allowance toward the darker fabric.*

4 *Using a rotary ruler, straighten the end. Then slice into eight segments 2½ inches wide.*

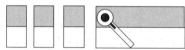

Sew these units together in pairs, with one unit rotated, as illustrated below, to complete the Four Patch unit.

The same principle may be applied to Nine Patch squares, or other combinations.

Half-square triangles

Half-square triangles are obtained by cutting a square in half along one diagonal. The straight grain of the fabric runs parallel to the short sides of the triangle.

The finished size of a half-square triangle is determined by the measurement of one of the short sides.

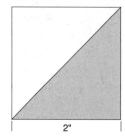

2"

The cut size of a half-square triangle is calculated by adding ⅞ inch to the finished size.

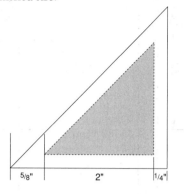

⅝"   2"   ¼"

Speed cutting half-square triangles

1 *For example: to the finished size of a 2-inch half-square triangle add seam allowances (⅝ inch + ¼ inch) or ⅞ inch for a cut size of 2⅞ inch.*
2 *Cut a 2⅞-inch strip of fabric. Slice into 2⅞-inch squares and then slice each square in half along one diagonal to obtain as many half-square triangles as required.*

Speed piecing half-square triangle units

The conventional method for producing half-square triangle units is to cut triangles from each fabric using templates, then to join each unit one by one. However, using the following method it is possible to produce 'ready-sewn' units - the grid facing will yield 12 such units at a time.

The contrasting fabrics are stitched right sides together in a grid pattern, then cut to reveal the units. (Note that the grid may be drafted directly onto the reverse of one of the fabrics, or a paper guide may be made.)

In the illustration (facing page), the solid lines represent cutting lines, and the dotted lines represent sewing lines.

1 *Calculate the cut size of the half-square triangle unit required for your design and on paper draft a 2-square x 3-square master grid to that dimension (the example illustrated is for 2-inch finished units).*
2 *Draw a diagonal line through each*

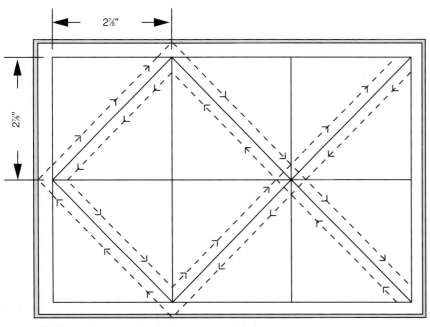

Half-square triangle grid for 2-inch finished units

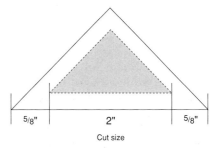

Cut size

square as illustrated (solid line). Refer to the illustration and draft a sewing line (dotted line) ¼ inch to either side of each diagonals.

3 From the two fabrics cut a rectangle slightly larger than the grid size. Copy the grid onto the reverse of one of the fabrics and place them right sides together. Alternatively, make a paper guide: trace off the lines from the master grid onto some tracing or light-weight paper to make a disposable paper guide. Centre the guide on the wrong side of the fabric and secure with some low-tack tape. It helps to stabilise the fabric layers by pinning them together outside the perimeter of the paper guide. Pin to secure, making sure that the pins do not obstruct the sewing line.

4 Reduce the machine stitch length slightly and sew the seam exactly on the sewing lines indicated following the direction of the arrows. By pivoting at the corners it is possible to complete the sewing with one seam only.

5 Cut into squares first, on the solid lines. Cut into triangles by cutting on the solid lines between the two sewing lines. Peel off the paper guide (if

used) by folding down and tearing off the seam allowance portion first, supporting the seam firmly between finger and thumb. Press the seams and trim the 'ears' that appear at the

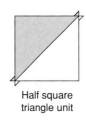

Half square
triangle unit

corner of the squares (see above). Each square of the grid produces two sets of half-square triangle units.

Quarter-square triangles

Quarter-square triangles are obtained by cutting a square into four across

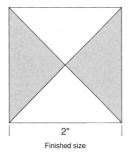

2"

Finished size

each diagonal. The long side is always on the straight grain.

The finished size of a quarter-square triangle is determined by the measurement of the long side. The cut size is calculated by adding 1¼ inches to the finished size (see illustration above).

Speed cutting quarter-square triangles

1 For example: to the finished size of a 2-inch quarter-square triangle add seam allowances (⅝ inch + ⅝ inch, or 1¼ inches) to determine the cut size of the triangle as 3¼ inches. Cut a 3¼-inch strip of fabric.

2 Slice into 3¼-inch squares and then slice each square into four across each diagonal

Speed piecing quarter-square triangle units

As with half-square triangles (see above) there is a very fast method of producing units using a stitched grid. The contrasting fabrics are stitched right sides together in a grid pattern, then cut to reveal the units. The grid below will yield 24 'ready sewn' units. (Note that the grid may be drafted directly onto the reverse of one of the fabrics, or a paper guide may be made.) In the illustration, the solid lines represent cutting lines, and the dotted lines represent sewing lines.

1 Calculate the cut size of a quarter-square triangle unit required for your design and on paper draft a 2-square x 3-square master grid to this size. Draw diagonal lines in each direction through every square. Sewing lines are drafted ¼ inch to either side of the diagonals running from top left to bottom right

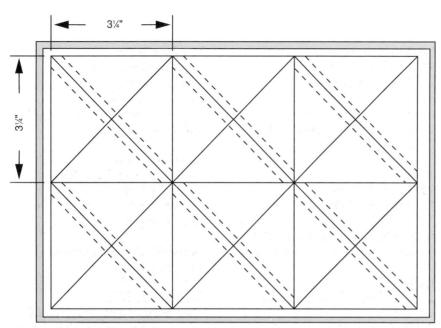

Quarter-square triangle grid for 2-inch finished units

(see illustration above).

2 *From the two fabrics cut a rectangle slightly larger than the grid size. Copy the grid onto the reverse of one of the fabrics and place them right sides together. Alternatively, make a paper guide: trace off the lines from the master grid onto some tracing or light-weight paper to make a disposable paper guide. Centre the guide on the wrong side of the fabric and secure with some low-tack tape. It helps to stabilise the fabric layers by pinning them together outside the perimeter of the paper guide. Pin to secure, making sure that the pins do not obstruct the sewing line.*

3 *Reduce the machine stitch length slightly and sew the seam exactly on the sewing lines indicated. Cut into squares first, along the solid lines, and then cut each square in half between the sewing lines and finally cut the quarter-square triangle units by cutting on the remaining line. Each square of the grid will produce four pairs of quarter-square triangles which are mirror images of each other.*

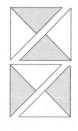

HINTS FOR SPEED CUTTING AND SEWING TECHNIQUES

- Remember the difference between cut and finished sizes

- Always use an accurate ¼-inch seam allowance

- Keep safety guards on all cutting equipment

- Always use a proper cutting mat

- Use spray starch on floppy fabric to make it easier to handle for cutting

- Keep your sewing machine well oiled and de-fluffed

- Replace burred machine needles immediately

SPECIALIST SUPPLIERS

Candle Makers' Supplies
28 Blythe Road, London W14 0HA.
Tel 0171 602 4031.
Shop and mail order: Procion MX cold
water fibre-reactive dyes, fabric paints.

Creative Grids
Leicester Laminating Services,
PO Box 207, Leicester LE3 6YP.
Tel 01162 857 151.
Mail order: template plastic and rotary
cutting equipment.

John Lewis Partnership
Department stores: fabrics, fabric
paints, cushion pads, fusible linings,
wadding and interlinings.

Kemtex Services Limited
Tameside Business Centre
Windmill Lane, Denton
Manchester M34 3QS.
Tel 0161 320 6505
Mail order: Procion MX cold water
fibre-reactive dyes, acid dyes, dye
chemicals and fabric paints.

Patchwork and Quilts
9 West Place, Wimbledon,
London SW19 4UH.
Tel 0181 946 1643
Shop and mail order: fabrics, gadgets,
books, specialist patchwork and
quilting supplies.

Piecemakers
13 Manor Green Road,
Epsom, Surrey KT19 8RA
Tel 01372 743161
Shop only. A selection of over 900
fabrics from USA, books and gadgets.

Quilt Basics
2 Meades Lane, Chesham, Bucks
HP4 1ND.
Tel 01494 785202.
Mail order: fabrics, patchwork and
quilting supplies.

The Quilt Room
Rear Carvilles, Station Road,
Dorking, Surrey RH4 1HQ.
Tel 01306 877307.
Mail order: fabrics, patchwork and
quilting supplies.

Strawberry Fayre
Chagford, Devon TQ13 8EN.
Tel 01647 433250.
Mail order: fabrics, patchwork and
quilting supplies.

George Weil & Sons Limited
18 Hanson Street,
London W1P 7DB.
Tel 0171 580 3763.
Shop and mail order: Procion MX
cold water fibre-reactive dyes, fabric
paints, cotton and silk fabrics.

PATCHWORK SOCIETIES

National Patchwork Association
PO Box 300, Heathersett, Norwich,
Norfolk NR9 3DB.

The Quilters' Guild
OP66, Dean Clough, Halifax,
West Yorkshire HX3 5AX.

American Quilters' Society
PO Box 3290 Paducah,
KY 42002-3290, USA.

SPECIALIST PUBLICATIONS

From societies:

American Quilter (American Quilters'
Society quarterly magazine).

Independent Patchworker (National
Patchwork Association UK quarterly
newsletter).

The Quilter (Quilters' Guild UK
quarterly newsletter).

From newsagents:

Patchwork and Quilting (Nexus Media
Communications Ltd, UK bi-monthly
magazine).

Popular Patchwork (Traplet
Publications, UK bi-monthly
magazine).

US publication:

Quilters' Newsletter Magazine (Leman
Publications Inc., 10 issues per year).

This book is dedicated
To my Grandmother Mary Ann Crosbie who taught me to sew and to my mother
Kitty Moloney who gave me life and whose indomitable spirit I shall always
cherish.

Acknowlegments
A big thank-you to all the members of the Garnet Publishing family who have
been so supportive and patient with me during the writing of this series. A very
special thank you to Jackie Jones for her thoughtful suggestions and great
tolerance. With gratitude also to my husband John for his patience and humour, to
Prue Bucknell for her confidence in my ability and to all my students for their
encouragement and generosity.

© 1996 Garnet Publishing Ltd
Text and illustrations © 1996 Pippa Abrahams

ISBN 1 85964 041 9

First edition

British Library Cataloguing-in-Publication Data.
A catalogue record for this book is available from the British Library.

Project management: Jackie Jones
Design: Mark Slader and David Rose
Photography: Simon Webb and Pippa Abrahams

Printed in Lebanon

Published by Garnet Publishing Ltd,
8 Southern Court, South Street,
Reading, RG1 4QS, UK

While every care has been taken in the preparation of this book, neither the
author nor publishers can accept any liability for any consequences arising from
the use of information contained herein.